PR ...

T...

The sequence of events as foretold is by no means certain. Public prophecy ceased with the death of St. John the Apostle. Private prophecy, even if received from God, is not reliable because the prophet is fallible. He can forget, misunderstand or misinterpret. Even when he does not err, those who hear him and who transmit the message can err.

So when we state here that this seems to be the general sequence of things foretold, it is largely merely a private opinion.

1. Before the Gospel is preached and accepted in all the world, there shall come world wars and insidious doctrines accompanied by widespread persecution.

2. This era shall be terminated by the direct interference of God destroying the evil system or persons responsible for the persecution; and through the leadership of a great civil ruler and a great spiritual leader, a period of peace will come during which the nations will hear and accept the true Faith.

3. A great apostasy will follow.

4. Antichrist will come and reign three and one half years. He will be destroyed by the direct intervention of Christ.

5. The Second Coming of Christ will follow, but by how long a time is unknown.

6. The trumpet will sound, the dead will arise and be judged.

7. The world will be destroyed by fire.

8. There will be new heavens and a new earth.

PROPHECY
FOR
TODAY

A Summary of the Catholic Tradition
Concerning the End-of-Time Era

By

EDWARD CONNOR

"But I am come to teach thee what things shall befall thy people in the latter days . . ."

—Daniel 10:14

TAN BOOKS AND PUBLISHERS, INC.
Rockford, Illinois 61105

Nihil Obstat: James H. Culleton
                   Censor Librorum

Imprimatur: ✠ A. J. Willinger, C.Ss.,D.D.
                   Bishop of Monterey-Fresno

Library of Congress Catalog Card No.: 83-70408.

ISBN: 0-89555-212-4.

Printed and bound in the United States of America.

TAN BOOKS AND PUBLISHERS, INC.
P.O. Box 424
Rockford, Illinois 61105

1984

Dedicated to
Our Lady of the Rosary of Fatima

"Show the things that are to come hereafter, and we shall know that ye are gods." (*Isaias* 41:23).

TABLE OF CONTENTS

Chapter 1

PROPHECY

Prophecy in General

Prophecy is a word of many meanings but it is commonly understood to mean *knowledge of the free future,* i.e., how God will act in the future, how man will use his free will in the future, and the events resulting from both. It is in this sense that the word is used in this volume.

A doctor outlining the course of a disease to a patient is not gifted with prophecy. Neither is an astronomer foretelling the year, month and day of a comet's return. They are dealing with scientific facts in which a given cause produces certain effects or some part of the universe acts in accordance with certain inviolable laws.

The free future is known only to God and those to whom He chooses to reveal it. Neither the angels (faithful or fallen), the saints, nor Our Lady herself know future events contingent upon God or man's use of free will—unless it is made known to them.

Because of its unique quality, prophecy has always been linked with miracles as a sign from God that a certain revelation is true. Thus our Blessed Lord made use of prophecy in two ways to prove His messianic and divine claims: He showed that He fulfilled all the prophecies of the Old Testament that had foretold His life in detail, while Himself making prophecies that were fulfilled both in His lifetime and generations later.

1

Biblical Prophecy

All prophecies found in the Bible have been fulfilled except those referring to the "last days."

The prophecies of the Old Testament pertained mainly to the Jewish people, the nations with whom they mingled, and to the coming Messiah. The unfulfilled prophecies relate to the signs preceding the Second Coming of Christ, the Last Judgment, and the "new heaven and earth," and are found mainly in the books of Isaias and Daniel.

In the four gospels we find many references to the last days by Our Lord, especially in the famous Eschatological Discourse. Other such prophecies are to be found in the epistles of St. Paul and St. Peter, and of course in the single prophetic book of the New Testament, the Apocalypse. These prophecies will be considered in their proper place.

Private Prophecy

In the centuries since the canon of sacred Scripture was determined, many saints and mystics have claimed the gift of prophecy. Since all such comes under the heading of private revelation, it is never binding upon the faithful to believe. No matter how great the saint, we have no guarantee that every word found in his or her writings is infallible, especially when it comes to prophecy. When the cause of a proposed saint is introduced in Rome and the steps leading to canonization are begun, the writings of the person are carefully examined to judge their content of holiness, and to see if there is anything in them contrary to Catholic doctrine. If such writings are approved for the Acts of Beatification, that is no guarantee that the Church accepts as authentic any prophecy found in them. It simply means that the prophecy has nothing in it contrary to faith or morals.

The extreme caution one should use in approaching all private revelation is graphically exemplified by the classic instances in which a saint has been proven wrong in his predictions. Thus St. Vincent Ferrer (1350-1419) went about preaching the coming of the Antichrist and the end of the world in his own generation!

Then, too, there is the ticklish problem of one saint contradicting another in a revelation. It is true we may err in applying both prophecies to the same event, or one or the other prophecy may have been tampered with, but both suppositions bolster more strongly the premise that all private prophecy must be approached with great caution.

On the other hand, if it should be wondered whether only saints and mystics are endowed with this gift, we have the words of Benedict XIV: "The recipients of prophecy may be angels, devils, men, women, children, heathens, or gentiles; nor is it necessary that a man should be gifted with any particular disposition in order to receive the light of prophecy provided his intellect and senses be adapted for making manifest the things which God reveals to him. Though moral goodness is most profitable to a prophet, yet it is not necessary in order to obtain the gift of prophecy." (*Heroic Virtue* III, 144:150).

It will be noted in reading private prophecy that a great many of those that threaten calamities to the human race—and do not necessarily refer to the last days—are conditional in quality. It is made clear that if man turns from his sins, returns to God, and does penance, the scourges will not fall. Such were the messages given by Our Lady at La-Salette and at Fatima, and by Our Lord to Blessed Anna Maria Taigi. A notable example of this is found in sacred Scripture itself when Jonas preached to the men of Ninive:

"'Yet forty days, and Ninive shall be destroyed.' And the men of Ninive believed in God, and they proclaimed a fast, and put on sackcloth from the greatest to the least . . . And

God saw their works, that they were turned from their evil way. And God had mercy with regard to the evil which He had said that He would do to them, and He did it not." (*Jonas* 3:4-5, 10).

It is well to remember this "conditional" qualification when reading such prophecies as those referring to the "heavenly scourge" and the three days darkness.

Questionable Prophecies

Certain prophets of the Middle Ages have enjoyed great fame, especially Mother Shipton (born c. 1486 in Yorkshire, England) and Nostradamus (born 1503, Provence, France).

Many are fond of quoting the prophecies of Mother Shipton in which she foretells automobiles, airplanes, submarines and radio, but they rarely quote her couplet:

"The world to an end shall come
In eighteen hundred and eighty one."

Nostradamus has never enjoyed a prominent position as a prophet in the eyes of the Church. Many of his 354 quatrains are based on astrology, and in some of them he seems to prophesy the downfall of the Church. One prediction in regard to the papacy states: "After the seat is held seventeen years, five shall change in the same length of years." Pius XI was the first pontiff to reign seventeen years (Feb. 1922 - Feb. 1939); his successor, Pope Pius XII, reigned nineteen years, thus eliminating the other four popes promised in the prophecy.

Nostradamus also wrote: "When St. George's day falls upon Good Friday; when St. Mark's falls on Easter; when St. John's falls on Corpus Christi; then the end of the war will arrive." These feasts concurred in 1943 and will not do so again until 2038. As we all know, World War II came to an end in 1945.

Others who spoke of events in a year that would have the same concurrence of feasts were:

Werdin d'Otrante (13th century): "The Pope will cross the sea in a year when the Feast of St. George falls on Good Friday, and St. Mark's Feast comes on Easter Sunday, and the Feast of St. Anthony falls on Pentecost and the Feast of St. John the Baptist falls on Corpus Christi."

St. Bridget of Sweden (died 1373): "When the Feast of St. Mark shall fall on Easter, the Feast of St. Anthony on Pentecost, and that of St. John on Corpus Christi, the whole world shall cry 'Woe.'"

Venerable Magdalene Porzat (died 1850): "In the year when Easter occurs on the Feast of St. Mark, Pentecost on the Feast of St. Anthony, and Corpus Christi occurs on the Feast of St. John the Baptist, then the world will cry: 'Woe! Woe! Woe!'"

The Holy Father did not cross the sea in 1943, and certainly the year did not seem more "woeful" than the years that preceded and followed it. Perhaps 2038 is the destined year.

In the last century a good deal of attention has been given to the so-called Pyramid Prophecy. It is claimed that those who designed and built the Great Pyramid of Cheops worked into it a prophetic history of all the centuries to come until the year 2000 A.D. The reasoning is involved, having to do with lengths of corridors, tunnels and chambers, etc. Proponents of the prophecy solemnly declared that the date November 27, 1939 "closed off the evil forces from interfering in the affairs of men." (Invasion of Poland had taken place two months earlier. World War II still had over five and one half years to go.) The date October 12, 1940 was also given as the time when "the forces of good have been given the upper hand over all forces of evil, unhappiness, poverty, ill health and disease." (This was a year before Pearl Harbor.)

Chapter 2

THE PROPHECY
OF ST. MALACHY

Few private prophecies have captured the popular imagination like that prophecy on the popes ascribed to St. Malachy O'Morgair, Archbishop of Armagh, Ireland, who died in 1148. Tradition has it that when Malachy visited Pope Innocent II in Rome in 1139, he was granted a vision of all the Holy Fathers of the future. He wrote down a description of each in two to four Latin words and gave the list to Innocent, who was deeply troubled at the time and who is said to have derived great comfort from the prophecy. Nothing more is heard of the list until 1590 when a Benedictine monk, Arnold de Wyon, discovered it in the Vatican archives. It was published, promoting a controversy that has continued to our day.

Since Malachy was a good friend of St. Bernard of Clairvaux (in whose arms he died), it is asked why the latter did not mention the prophecy in his famous *Life of St. Malachy*. Why was the list lost for so many years? Of the 112 popes described in the prophecy, 74 had already reigned when the list was discovered, and opponents of the prophecy claim that the descriptions of these are far more exact than those of subsequent pontiffs. Was not the list the work of a forger who simply used hindsight to describe the popes of the preceding 450 years, and clever ambiguity for the popes of the future?

Proponents of the prophecy, however, stand on the fact that the prophetic utterances did fit all the popes *after* 1590 with uncanny aptness. Here are some in detail:

Clement XIII (reigned 1758-1769) is described as *Rosa Umbriae* ("The Rose of Umbria.") This pontiff had been governor of Rieti in Umbria, and the symbol of that district was a rose.

His successor, Clement XIV (1769-1774), appears as *Ursus Velox* ("The Nimble Bear.") His coat of arms showed a bear in flight.

The next pontiff, Pius VI (1775-1799), is described as *Peregrinus Apostolicus* ("The Apostolic Wanderer.") During his reign, this pope went to Germany to confer with the Emperor Joseph II. In the last years of his pontificate, he was forced by revolutionaries to flee Rome. After an arduous journey over the Alps, he died in Valence, France!

His successor was Pius VII (1800-1823), and he appears on Malachy's list as *Aquila Rapax* ("The Rapacious Eagle.") Since this pope was the most gentle and dove-like of men, the inscription has presented difficulties which some have tried to circumvent by applying the prophecy to Napoleon at whose hands Pius suffered so much.

The prophecy for Gregory XVI (1831-1846) reads *De Balneis Etruriae* ("From Balnea in Etruria.") This pontiff belonged to the religious order of Camaldoli, whose seat is at Balnea in Etruria.

Coming to the popes of the last century: Pius IX (1846-1878) *Crux de Cruce* ("Cross from a Cross.") The House of Savoy, which caused this pope so much suffering, had a cross on its coat of arms.

Leo XIII (1878-1903): *Lumen in Caelo* ("Light in the Heavens.") His coat of arms showed a shooting star.

Pius X (1903-1914): *Ignis Ardens* ("Burning Fire.")

Benedict XV (1914-1922): Pope of the first World War: *Religio Depopulata* ("Religion Devastated.")

Pius XI (1922-1939): *Fides Intrepida* ("Intrepid Faith.")

Pius XII (1939-1958): *Pastor Angelicus* ("The Angelic Shepherd.")

John XXIII (1958-1963): *Pastor et Nauta* ("The Shepherd and the Sailor.") Since he was formerly Patriarch of Venice, this pontiff came from a city of canals.

Paul VI (1963-1978): *Flos Florum* ("The Flower of Flowers.") His coat of arms displayed the fleur-de-lis.

John Paul I (1978-1978): *De Medietate Lunae* ("From the Half of the Moon.") The first two letters of his family name, Luciani, form half of "luna," the Latin word for "moon."

John Paul II (1978-   ): *De Labore Solis* ("From the Labor of the Sun.")

Only two more popes remain on Malachy's list:

De Gloria Olivae ("From the Glory of the Olive") and *Petrus Romanus* ("Peter the Roman.")

The prophecy concludes: "In the final persecution of the Holy Roman Church there shall reign Peter the Roman who will feed his flock amid many tribulations, after which the seven-hilled city will be destroyed and the terrible judge will judge the people."

However, there is no inference that there might not be other pontiffs between "From the Glory of the Olive" and "Peter the Roman."

Mention might also be made of the Monk of Padua who in 1740 added his own observations to the prophecies of Malachy, even indicating which name each future pope would take. In this regard he was correct until Benedict XV, who, according to the Monk, was to be Paul VI. Pius XII was also incorrectly designated as Gregory XVII, while John XXIII, Paul VI, John Paul I and John Paul II were erroneously called Paul VII, Clement XV, Pius XII and Gregory XVIII. Thus it appears the Monk of Padua is discredited as a prophet, unless we are to suppose that the later part of his work is a forgery.

Malachy's complete list is given in Appendix A. A study of the entire prophecy shows that fulfillment is made possible only by including anti-popes—almost a death blow to the integrity of the prophecy since Malachy's vision of all popes of the future could hardly have included those who were not to be pope at all, and Innocent II would not have derived much "comfort" from a prophecy involving ten anti-popes. We are also presented with the unique problem of John XXIII appearing *twice* on Malachy's list: No. 50, "Stag of the Siren," and No. 107, "Shepherd and the Sailor."

Chapter 3

THE SECRETS OF
LA SALETTE AND FATIMA

On September 19, 1846 Our Blessed Lady appeared weeping to two children, Melanie Matthieu, 15, and Maximin Giraud, 11, on the holy mountain of La Salette in southeastern France. Through these children, Our Lady gave a message to the people of France beginning, "If my people will not submit, I shall be forced to let go the hand of my Son. It is so strong, so heavy that I can no longer withhold it. For how long a time do I suffer for you. If I would not have my Son abandon you I am compelled to pray to Him without ceasing."

Our Lady went on to tell of the crop failures, famine and starvation that would afflict the French people for their continued breaking of the Second and Third Commandments of God.

In the middle of the message she gave each of the children a "secret" which the other did not hear. In 1851 the children agreed to make these secrets known to the Holy Father, Pius IX, and wrote them out in the presence of distinguished clerics and laymen.

Maximin wrote his secret in seven paragraphs—each numbered—with the heading: "Most Holy Father, on the 19th of September 1846 a Lady appeared to me; they say it is the Blessed Virgin; you will judge whether it was by what follows." While writing, the boy asked the bystanders how to spell "pontiff."

When Melanie wrote her secret (of considerably greater

11

length than the boy's), she asked the meaning of the words "infallibly" and "Antichrist."

When the messages were presented in Rome, Pope Pius opened Maximin's first and said, "Here is all the candor and simplicity of a child." While reading Melanie's secret, the pontiff appeared deeply moved and disturbed. He said, "These are scourges with which France is threatened but she is not alone culpable. Germany, Italy, all Europe is culpable and merits chastisement. I have less to fear from open impiety than from indifference and human respect. It is not without reason that the Church is called militant, and here"—indicating himself—"you behold its captain." He concluded, "I must read these letters more at leisure."

Years later, the Superior General of the Missionaries of Our Lady of La Salette asked Pius if anything might be revealed about the secrets. The pontiff answered, "You wish to know the secrets of La Salette. Well, here are the secrets of La Salette: Unless you do penance you shall all perish."

In 1879 (according to the *Catholic Encyclopedia*) Melanie published her secret, but students of La Salette doubt that the published message is the same as that received from Our Lady in 1846. They claim that Melanie's thinking was colored from having read a great deal of apocalyptic literature. In any event, many different versions of Melanie's secret appeared throughout France and Europe, causing a great deal of confusion and scandal until December 21, 1915 the Sacred Congregation of the Holy Office in Rome issued a decree stating: "It has come to the knowledge of this Supreme Congregation that there are still persons, even ecclesiastics, who, in spite of the answers and decisions of the Sacred Congregation itself, continue by books, pamphlets and articles published in periodicals, whether signed or anonymous, to discuss the question of the Secrets of La Salette, its various texts, its adaptations to our present times or to the future, and these, not only without the approbation of their Bishops, but even in spite of their express prohibition. In order that these abuses, which are harmful to true piety, and seriously attack ecclesiastical authority, may be repressed, the same Sacred Congregation orders the faithful of all countries to abstain from treating and discussing this said question, under whatsoever pretext or form, either in books, pamphlets or articles signed or anonymous, or in any other way."

After stating the penalties the transgressors will incur, the decree concludes: "This Decree is not, however, contrary to the devotion of the Blessed Virgin invoked and known under the title of Reconciler of La Salette."

Fatima

On July 13, 1917 Our Lady gave the three children of Fatima a secret message and commanded them to tell it to no one. Ten years later (two of the children having died) Lucy dos Santos received permission from Heaven to reveal part of this secret. She made it known to her confessors, to the Bishop of Leiria, the Mother Provincial of the Dorothean Sisters and the Reverend Joseph Galamba. However, the bishop did not think it prudent to publish the secret until 1942, on the occasion of the 25th anniversary of the sun miracle of Fatima. Even so, the text was changed and "consecration of Russia" became "consecration of the world" in order that Portugal would not seem to be violating her neutrality in World War II. Lucy has corrected the text on several occasions so that now we have a fully authentic version.

The secret was in three distinct parts, and Lucy received permission to reveal the first two. The third part was written down, placed in a sealed envelope and given to the Bishop of Leiria to be opened and read in the year 1960.[1]

The first part of the secret was a terrifying vision of Hell and the following message from Our Lady:

"You have seen Hell where the souls of poor sinners go. To save them, God wishes to establish in the world devotion to my Immaculate Heart.

"If people do what I shall tell you, many souls will be saved and there will be peace.

"The war is going to end, but if people do not stop offending God another and worse one will begin in the reign of Pius XI. When you shall see a night illuminated by an unknown light, know that it is the great sign God is giving you that He is going to punish the world for its sins by means of war, famine, and persecution of the Church and the Holy Father.

"To prevent it I shall come to ask for the consecration of Russia to my Immaculate Heart and Communions of reparation on the first Saturdays.

"If they heed my requests, Russia will be converted and there will be peace. Otherwise Russia will spread her errors throughout the world, promoting wars and persecution of the Church; the good will be martyred, the Holy Father will have much to suffer, various nations will be annihilated.

"But in the end my Immaculate Heart shall triumph. The Holy Father will consecrate Russia to me, she will be converted, and a certain period of peace will be given to the world.

"In Portugal the dogma of Faith will always be kept."

The second part of the secret referred to the devotion to the Immaculate Heart of Mary.

Our Lady told of five scourges that would fall upon the world if mankind did not repent and return to God, and she gave a sign by which it might be known that the punishments were at hand: "When you shall see a night illuminated by an unknown light."

This sign came on the night of January 25, 1938 when all Europe and part of North America were lighted up by an extraordinary appearance of the aurora borealis, better known as the northern lights. The story of the great light and the fear and terror it inspired everywhere was reported by all leading newspapers, appearing on the front page of the *New York Times.* From her convent cell in Spain, Lucy recognized the light as the sign and made it known to her bishop.[2]

The five scourges were to be:

1. A second world war beginning in the reign of Pius XI (in his pontificate we had the Chinese-Japanese war, the Spanish civil war, and the annexation of Austria—all of which might be considered the prologue to World War II);

2. The rise and success of Russian Communism;

3. The martyrdom of the faithful;

4. The Holy Father having much to suffer;

5. The annihilation of nations.

The first four punishments have come to pass. The fifth has not—if the prophecy is to be taken literally[3]—and can still be avoided if the faithful will fulfill Our Lady's requests for penance, daily Rosary, and devotion to her Immaculate Heart.

In the secret Our Lady said she would return to ask for the consecration of Russia to her Immaculate Heart. She appeared to Lucy in 1929 and asked that on one certain day the Holy Father, in union with all the bishops in the world, consecrate Russia to her Immaculate Heart.

Later, in an intimate conversation, Our Lord complained to Lucy, saying: "They did not wish to heed My request. Like the King of France, they will repent and do it, but it will be late. Russia will have already spread her errors throughout the world, provoking wars and persecutions of the Church; the Holy Father will have much to suffer."

On October 31, 1942 Pius XII consecrated the world and Russia to the Immaculate Heart. On July 6, 1952 he consecrated Russia specifically. Pope Paul VI consecrated the world to Our Lady's Immaculate Heart in 1964. On May 13, 1982 Pope John Paul II, uniting himself in intention with the world's bishops, consecrated the world, with a particular mention of Russia, to the Immaculate Heart of Mary. ("In a particular way we entrust and consecrate to thee those individuals and nations which particularly need to be entrusted and consecrated.") On March 24-25, 1984 Pope John Paul II renewed this consecration, asking the bishops of the world to join with him in making the consecration from their own dioceses. When he pronounced the Act of Consecration in Rome, the Holy Father unexpectedly added these significant words: "Enlighten especially the peoples whose consecration and entrustment by us you are awaiting."

The scourges foretold at Fatima were conditional, but the prophecy of Russia's conversion was not. It was *absolute*, according to Lucy, but its exact time depends on the prayers and penances of the faithful.

NOTES

1. What happened in 1960 is still in doubt. In any event, the last part of the secret was never officially published.
2. Despite the fact that Lucy considered this light the one she expected, she is not to be considered infallible in the matter. It will also be noted that the text of the secret says "an unknown light," whereas this light is definitely identified as "aurora borealis."
3. Latvia and Estonia are said to have disappeared.

Chapter 4

THE EARTHLY SCOURGE,
THE HEAVENLY SCOURGE AND
THE THREE DAYS DARKNESS

Many are the prophecies which tell of a series of terrible wars before the end of time, and if mankind persists in its path away from God, something far worse: a heavenly scourge in which God will no longer act through secondary causes but will Himself directly punish the wicked and purify the world.

The Earthly Scourge—
World War I and World War II

Telesphorus of Cozensa (died 1388): "Terrible wars among nations of Europe will follow the secularization of Church property."

Old German (12th century): "A great war will come, after which the Kaiser will leave the country. Troubled times will follow, although the land is at peace. Then a man of lowly birth will come into power and win many successes so that Germany will become 'Great Germany.' There will be few Jews in the country. When at the height of his power, this man will do something to cause another world war, resulting in Germany's downfall. Germany will become small again, but under a Catholic monarch will regain power and prestige."

Saint Odile (died 740): "Listen, listen, O my brother, for I have seen the terror of the forests and of the mountains. Fear has seized the people because never in any region of the universe has one given testimony of such trouble. The time has come when Germany will be called the most belligerent nation of the world. The period has arrived when out of her bosom will come the terrible warrior who will undertake to spread war in the world. The men in arms will call him the Antichrist. He will be cursed by mothers by the thousands who will lament like Rachel over the fate of their children, and who will refuse consolation because they will no longer be of this world and all will be devastated in their homes.

"The conqueror will come from the banks of the Danube. He will be a remarkable chief among men. The war that he will make will be the most terrifying that men have ever undertaken. His army will be flamboyant and the helmets of his soldiers will bear points darting flashlights, while their hands will carry lighted torches. It will be impossible to calculate the number of cruelties committed. He will be victorious on land, sea, and even in the air because one will see winged warriors, in these unbelievable attacks, mounting to the heavens to seize the stars and throw them on the cities from one end of the universe to the other in order to start gigantic fires. The nations will be astonished and will say: 'Whence comes this force?' 'How is he able to undertake a war?' The earth will tremble at the shock of the fighting. The rivers will run red with blood and sea monsters will disperse with terror to the top of the oceans, while black storms will spread desolation everywhere. Future generations will be astonished to see that his powerful and numerous enemies will not have been capable of stopping the march of his victories.

"And the war will be long. The conqueror will have attained the apogee of his triumphs towards the middle of the sixth month of the second year of hostilities. This will be the end of the first period of bloody victories. He will say, 'Accept the yoke of my domination,' while continuing his victories. But his enemies will not submit and the war will continue and he will cry out, 'Misfortune will make them fall because I am the conqueror.'

"The second part of the war will be equal in length to half the first part!¹ They will call it the period of 'diminution.' It will be full of surprises which will make the earth tremble when twenty belligerent nations will clash. Toward the middle of this period the little nations submissive to the conqueror will cry out, 'Give us peace.' But there will not be peace for these nations. This will not be the end of these wars but the beginning of the end, and the combats of body against body will take place in the citadel of citadels. Then will see a revolt among the women of his own country, who will wish to stone him. But one will also see prodigies in the Orient.

"The third period will be the shortest of all and the conqueror will have lost confidence in his warriors. This period will be called the 'period of invasion' because by just retribution the soil of the conqueror, by reason of his injustice and his atheism, will be invaded in all parts and pillaged. Around the mountains, torrents of blood will flow. This will be then the last battle.

"The nations will sing hymns of gratitude in the temples of God and will thank the Most High for their deliverance because then will have appeared the warrior who will disperse the troops of the conqueror, the armies of which will be annihilated by an unknown and frightful illness. This evil will discourage his soldiers, while the nations will say: 'The finger of God is there. It is a just chastisement.'

"Because God is just—while sometimes allowing cruelty and depredations—all the spoliated people, who will have believed Him, will recover what they have lost and something additional as a reward on earth."

Mathew Lang (died 1820): "After the great war (World War I) there will be no peace. The people will rise and all will fight against each other . . . The rich and nobles will be killed. The world war will not make people better but much worse . . . Tell your children that their children will live to see the time when the earth will be cleared. God will do away with people because there will be no charity among men. Religious faith will decline; priests will not be respected; people will be intent only on eating and drinking; there will be immensely rich people and large numbers of paupers; great wealth will not endure long, for the red caps (Communists?) will come. People will hide in the forests and many will go into exile. After this civil conflict and general cleaning-up people will love each other as much as previously they hated one another."

Teresa Neumann (September 6, 1936) (words of Our Lord): "The provocations have in these days attained their height. The furies of Hell rage now. The chastisement of God is inevitable. Every future petition to help them, to spare them, displeases Me. If you petition Me for the conversion of dying sinners in the last hour I will hear you. No! Do not petition Me to prevent this chastisement. Until now victims (many of whom existed in many parishes) have offered their merits to expiate for the crimes of mankind, which held back the wrath of God, but now their expiations are not enough and the chastisement is now certain and unpreventable. It will happen suddenly. Fortunate are those who already are in their graves. I have warned them and have postponed, as I did with Sodom, but Sodom would not listen to Me, nor do the people listen to Me nowadays, nor heed My warnings; therefore they will incur the sad experience of My wrath which they deserve."

The Heavenly Scourge

Blessed Anna Maria Taigi (died 1837): "God will ordain two punishments: one, in the form of wars, revolutions and other evils, will originate on earth; the other will be sent from Heaven."

"First, several earthly scourges will come. They are going to be dreadful, but they will be mitigated and shortened by the prayers and penances of many holy souls. There will be great wars in which millions of people will perish through iron. But after these earthly scourges will come the heavenly one, which will be directed solely against the impenitent. This scourge will be far more frightful and terrible; it will be mitigated by nothing, but it will take place and act in its full rigor."

Venerable Maria of Agreda (died 1665): "An unusual chastisement of the human race will take place toward the end of the world."

Sister Marianne (died 1804): "So long as public prayers will be made, nothing shall happen; but a time will come when public prayers shall cease. People will say, 'Things will remain as they are.' It is then that the great calamity shall occur. This great calamity shall consist in:
1. a great flight;
2. great tribulations in many large cities of France;
3. a horrible massacre in the capital, namely, Paris.

"During the battle, people shall hear the noise of the cannon nine leagues distant.

"Before the great combat the wicked shall be masters. They will perpetrate all the evils in their power, but not as much as they desire, because they shall not have the time. Good and faithful Catholics, less in number, shall be on the point of being annihilated, but a stroke from Heaven shall save them.

"O power of God! O power of God! All the wicked shall perish, and also many good men. O, how frightful shall these calamities be! The churches shall be closed, but only for the space of twenty-four hours. Religious women, being terrified, shall be on the point of abandoning the convent, but they shall remain. At this time such extraordinary events shall take place that the most incredulous will be forced to say, 'The finger of God is there.' O power of God! There shall be a terrible night during which no one shall be able to sleep. These trials shall not last long because no person could endure them. When all shall appear lost, all will be saved. It is then that dispatches shall arrive announcing good news, when the *Te Deum* shall be sung in a manner in which it has never been heard before. It is then that the Prince shall reign, whom people will seek that before did not esteem him. At that time the triumph of religion will be so great that no one has ever seen the equal. All injustices will be repaired, civil laws will be formed in harmony with the laws of God and of the Church. The instruction given to children will be most Christian; pious guilds for workmen shall be reestablished; the triumph of the Church and of France shall be most glorious."

Elizabeth Canori-Mora (died 1825): "All men shall rise one against the other, and they shall kill one another without pity. During this sanguinary conflict the avenging arm of God will strike the wicked, and in His mighty power He will punish their pride and presumption. God will employ the powers of Hell for the extermination of these impious and heretical persons who desire to overthrow the Church and destroy it to its very foundation. These presumptuous men in their mad impiety believe that they can overthrow God from His throne; but the Lord will despise these artifices, and through an effect of His Mighty Hand He will punish these impious blasphemers by giving permission to the infernal spirits to come out from Hell. Innumerable legions of demons shall overrun the earth, and shall execute the orders of Divine Justice by causing terrible calamities and disasters; they shall attack everything; they shall injure individual persons and entire families; they shall devastate property and alimentary productions, cities and villages. Nothing on earth shall be spared. God will allow the demons to strike with death those impious men because they gave themselves up to the infernal powers and had formed with them a compact against the Catholic Church.

"Being desirous of more fully penetrating my spirit with a deeper sentiment of His Divine Justice, God showed to me the awful abyss; I saw in the bowels of the earth a dark and frightening cavern, whence an infinite number of demons were issuing forth, who under the form of men and beasts came to ravage the earth, leaving everywhere ruins and blood. Happy will be all true and good Catholics! They shall experience the powerful protection of the holy Apostles, Saint Peter and Saint Paul, who will watch over them lest they may be injured either in their persons or their property. Those evil spirits shall plunder every place where God has been outraged, despised, and blasphemed; the edifices they profaned will be pulled down and destroyed, and nothing but ruins shall remain of them.

"After this frightful punishment I saw the Heavens opening and Saint Peter coming down again upon earth; he was vested in his pontifical robes, and surrounded by a great number of angels, who were chanting hymns in his honor, and they proclaimed him as sovereign of the earth. I saw also Saint Paul descending upon the earth. By God's command he traversed the earth and chained the demons whom he brought before Saint Peter, who commanded them to return into Hell whence they had come.

"Then a great light appeared upon the earth which was the sign of the reconciliation of God with man. The angels conducted before the throne of the prince of the Apostles the small flock that had remained faithful to Jesus Christ.

These good and zealous Christians testified to him the most profound respect, praising God and thanking the Apostles for having delivered them from the common destruction, and for having protected the Church of Jesus Christ by not permitting her to be infected with the false maxims of the world. Saint Peter then chose the new pope. The Church was again organized; religious orders were reestablished; the private families of ordinary Christians, through their great fervor and zeal for the glory of God, became like the most exemplary communities. Such is the glorious triumph reserved for the Catholic Church; she shall be praised, honored and esteemed by all men. All men shall become Catholics, and shall acknowledge the Pope as Vicar of Jesus Christ."

Nursing Nun of Belez (died 1830): "There will be a great slaughtering whereby the wicked will try to eradicate the religion of Jesus Christ. After they have killed a great number they will raise a cry of victory, but suddenly the good will receive help from above. This great crisis, in which the good will eventually triumph, will be of short duration, namely about three months. The majority of the wicked will perish and the living will be very much afraid over the chastisement of the others. They cannot but recognize the finger of God and adore His omnipotence. Many will then be converted and justice restored."

Father Bernard Maria Clausi, O.F.M. (died 1849): "Before the triumph of the Church comes, God will first take vengeance on the wicked, especially against the godless. It will be a new judgment; the like has never been seen before, and it will be universal. It will be so terrible that those who outlive it will imagine that they are the only ones spared. All people will then be good and contrite. The judgment will come suddenly and be of short duration. Then comes the triumph of the Church and the reign of brotherly love.

Happy indeed they who live to see those blessed days. However, before that, evil will have made such progress that it will look like all the devils of Hell were let loose on earth, so terrible will be the persecution of the wicked against the just, who will have to suffer true martyrdom."

Abbess Maria Steiner (died 1862): "I see the Lord as He will be scourging the world and chastising it in a fearful manner so that few men and women will remain. The monks will have to leave their monasteries, and the nuns will be driven from their convents, especially in Italy . . . The Holy Church will be persecuted . . . Unless people obtain pardon through their prayers, the time will come when they will see the sword and death, and Rome will be without a shepherd.

"The Lord showed me how beautiful the world will be like after the awful chastisement. The people will be like the Christians of the primitive Church."

Mother Alphonse Eppinger (1867): "After God has purified the world, faith and peace will return. Whole nations will adhere to the teachings of the Catholic Church."

Pope Pius IX (died 1878): "Since the whole world is against God and His Church, it is evident that He has reserved the victory over His enemies to Himself. This will be more obvious when it is considered that the root of all our present evils is to be found in the fact that those with talents and vigor crave earthly pleasures and not only desert God but repudiate Him altogether; thus it appears they cannot be brought back to God in any other way except through an act that cannot be ascribed to any secondary agency, and thus all will be forced to look to the supernatural and cry out: 'From the Lord is this come to pass and it is wonderful in our eyes.' . . . There will come a great wonder which will fill the world with astonishment. This wonder will be preceded by the triumph of revolution. The Church will suffer exceedingly. Her servants and her chieftain will be mocked, scourged and martyred."

The Three Days Darkness

Blessed Anna Maria Taigi (died 1837): "There shall come over all the earth an intense darkness lasting three days and three nights. Nothing will be visible and the air will be laden with pestilence, which will claim principally but not exclusively the enemies of religion. During this darkness artificial light will be impossible. Only blessed candles can be lighted and will afford illumination. He who out of curiosity opens his window to look out or leaves his house will fall dead on the spot. During these three days the people should remain in their homes, pray the Rosary and beg God for mercy.

"On this terrible occasion so many of these wicked men—enemies of His Church and of their God—shall be killed by this divine scourge that their corpses round Rome will be as numerous as the fish which a recent inundation of the Tiber had carried into the city. All the enemies of the Church, secret as well as known, will perish over the whole earth during that universal darkness, with the exception of some few, whom God will soon after convert. The air shall be infected with demons, who will appear under all sorts of hideous forms.

"After the three days of darkness Saints Peter and Paul, having come down from Heaven, will preach throughout the world and designate a new pope. A great light will flash from their bodies and will settle upon the cardinal, the future Pontiff. Then Christianity will spread throughout the world. Whole nations will join the Church shortly before the reign of the Antichrist. These conversions will be amazing. Those who shall survive shall have to conduct themselves well. There shall be innumerable conversions of heretics, who will return to the bosom of the Church; all will note the edifying conduct of their lives, as well as that of all other Catholics. Russia, England and China will come into the Church."

Saint Caspar del Bufalo (died 1837). He foretold "the destruction of impenitent persecutors of the Church during the three days darkness. To him who outlives the darkness and fear of the three days, it will seem as if he were alone on earth because the world will be covered everywhere with carcasses."

Sister Rose Asdenti (1847). She foretold the three days darkness and that England would return to the unity of faith.

Palma Maria d'Oria (died 1863): "There shall be a three days darkness, during which the atmosphere will be infected by innumerable devils, who shall cause the death of large multitudes of unbelievers and wicked men. Blessed candles alone shall be able to give light and preserve the faithful Catholics from this impending dreadful scourge. Supernatural prodigies shall appear in the heavens. There is to be a short but furious war, during which the enemies of religion and mankind shall be universally destroyed. A general pacification of the world and the universal triumph of the Church are to follow."

Sister Mary of Jesus Crucified of Pau (died 1878): "All states will be shaken by war and civil conflict. During a darkness lasting three days the people given to evil ways will perish so that only one fourth of mankind will survive. The clergy too will be greatly reduced in number, as most of them will die in defense of the Faith or their country."

Marie Julie Jahenny of La Fraudais (1891): "There will come three days of continued darkness. The blessed candle of wax alone will give light during the horrid darkness. One candle will last for three days, but in the houses of the godless they will *not* give light. During those three days the demons will appear in abominable and horrible forms; they will make the air resound with shocking blasphemies. The lightning will penetrate the homes, but will not extinguish the light of the blessed candles; neither wind nor storm nor earthquake will extinguish it. Red clouds like blood will pass in the sky, the crash of thunder will make the earth tremble; lightning will flash through the streets at an unusual time of the year; the earth will tremble to its foundations; the ocean will cast its foaming waves over the land; the earth will be changed to an immense cemetery; the corpses of the wicked and the just will cover the face of the earth. The famine that follows will be great. All vegetation will be destroyed as well as three fourths of the human race. The crisis will come all of a sudden and chastisement will be worldwide."

NOTES

1. From this point, the prophecy is less exact in its application to World War II, and may refer in part to World War II and in part to some consequent struggle.

Chapter 5

THE GREAT MONARCH
AND THE ANGELIC PASTOR

The prophecies in the preceding chapter told not only of
the scourges that have fallen upon mankind and those that
may yet fall, but also of the purification of the world and of
a golden age for the Church that will follow. Private revelation has many references to two personages who will play
joint pre-eminent roles in these events: the Great Monarch
and the Angelic Pastor (or Angelic Shepherd). Curiously
enough, there are far more prophecies referring to the
former than to the latter, and they go as far back as the third
century. If the prophecy of St. Malachy be true, then the
late Pius XII *was* the *"Pastor Angelicus,"* though his na-
tionality and pontificate did not fit the details of the
prophecies, and there is still no sign to date of the appearance of the Great Monarch. Some have taken Don
Bosco's prediction, "The Pope will die and live again," to
mean that Pius XII was not the Angelic Shepherd, but a
continuation, as it were, of Pius XI, who was "Intrepid
Faith." They point, furthermore, to several prophecies that
seem to indicate a succession of three, four, or five popes as
Angelic Pastors. With such verbal juggling one can, of
course, make out a prophecy to mean anything desired.

Saint Hippolytus (died 235): "The Great French Monarch
who shall subject all the East shall come around the end of
the world."

Saint Cataldus of Tarentino (c. 500): "The Great Monarch will be in war till he is forty years of age; a king of the House of Lily, he will assemble great armies and expel tyrants from his empire. He will conquer England and other island empires. Greece he will invade and be made a king thereof. Clochis, Cyprus, the Turks and barbarians he will subdue and have all men to worship the Crucified One. He will at length lay down his crown in Jerusalem."

Saint Caesar of Arles (469-543): "When the entire world, and in a special manner France, and in France more particularly the provinces of the North, of the East, and above all that of Lorraine and Champagne, shall have been a prey to the greatest miseries and trials, then the provinces shall be succored by a prince who had been exiled in his youth, and who shall recover the crown of the lilies.

"This prince shall extend his dominion over the entire universe. At the same time there will be a Great Pope, who will be most eminent in sanctity and most perfect in every quality. This Pope shall have with him the Great Monarch, a most virtuous man, who shall be a scion of the holy race of the French kings. This Great Monarch will assist the Pope in the reformation of the whole earth. Many princes and nations that are living in error and impiety shall be converted, and an admirable peace shall reign among men during many years because the wrath of God shall be appeased through repentance, penance and good works. There will be one common law, one only faith, one baptism, one religion. All nations shall recognize the Holy See of Rome, and shall pay homage to the Pope. But after some considerable time fervor shall cool, iniquity shall abound, and moral corruption shall become worse than ever, which shall bring upon mankind the last and worst persecution of Antichrist and the end of the world."

Blessed Rabanus Maurus (died 856): "Our principal doctors

agree in announcing to us that toward the end of time one of the descendants of the kings of France shall reign over all the Roman empire, and that he shall be the greatest of the French monarchs, and the last of his race.

"After having most happily governed his kingdom, he will go to Jerusalem, and depose on Mount Olivet his scepter and crown. This shall be the end and conclusion of the Roman and Christian Empire."

Monk Adso (died 992): "Some of our teachers say that a King of the Franks will possess the entire Roman Empire. This King will be the greatest and last of all monarchs, and after having prosperously governed his kingdom he will come in the end to Jerusalem and he will lay down his scepter and his crown upon the Mount of Olives. This will be the end and consummation of the Empire of Rome, and immediately afterwards Antichrist will come."

Chronicle of Magdeburg (12th century?): "Of the blood of the Emperor Charles the Great and the King of France shall arise an Emperor named Charles, who shall rule imperially in Europe, by whom the decayed estate of the Church shall be reformed and the ancient glory of the Empire again restored."

Aystinger the German (12th century?): "There shall arise in the last times a Prince sprung from the Emperor Charles who shall recover the land of promise and reform the Church. He shall be the Emperor of Europe."

Abbot "Merlin" Joachim (died 1202): "After many prolonged sufferings endured by Christians, and after a too great effusion of innocent blood, the Lord shall give peace and happiness to the desolated nations. A remarkable Pope will be seated on the pontifical throne, under the special protection of the angels. Holy and full of gentleness, he shall undo all wrong, he shall recover the states of the Church, and reunite the exiled temporal powers. He shall be revered by all people, and shall recover the kingdom of Jerusalem. As the only Pastor he shall reunite the Eastern to the Western Church, and thus only one faith will be in vigor. The sanctity of this beneficent Pontiff will be so great that the highest potentates shall bow down before his presence. This holy man shall crush the arrogance of religious schism and heresy. All men will return to the primitive Church, and there shall be only one pastor, one law, one master—humble, modest, and fearing God. The true God of the Jews, our Lord Jesus Christ, will make everything prosper beyond all human hope, because God alone can and will pour down on the wounds of humanity the oily balm of sweetness . . .

"This holy Pope shall be both pastor and reformer. Through him the East and West shall be in everlasting concord. The city of Babylon shall then be the head and guide of the world. Rome, weakened in temporal power, shall forever preserve her spiritual dominion, and shall enjoy great peace. During these happy days the Angelic Pope shall be able to address to Heaven prayers full of sweetness. The dispersed nation (Jews) shall also enjoy tranquillity. Six and a half years after this time the Pope will render his soul to God. The end of his days shall arrive in an arid province, situated between a river and a lake near the mountains . . .

"At the beginning, in order to obtain these happy results, having need of a powerful assistance, this holy Pontiff will ask the cooperation of the generous monarch of France (Great Monarch). At that time a handsome monarch, a scion of King Pepin, will come as a pilgrim to witness the splendor of this glorious Pontiff, whose name shall begin with R . . . A temporal throne becoming vacant, the Pope shall place on it this king whose assistance he shall ask . . .

"A man of remarkable sanctity will be his successor in

the Pontifical chair. Through him God will work so many prodigies that all men shall revere him, and no person will dare to oppose his precepts. He shall not allow the clergy to have many benefices. He will induce them to live by the tithes and offerings of the faithful. He shall interdict pomp in dress, and all immorality in dances and songs. He will preach the gospel in person, and exhort all honest ladies to appear in public without any ornament of gold or precious stones. After having occupied the Holy See for a long period of time he shall happily return to the Lord.

"His three immediate successors shall be men of exemplary holiness. One after the other will be models of virtue, and shall work miracles, confirming the teaching of their predecessors. Under their government the Church shall spread, and these Popes shall be called the Angelic Pastors."

Werdin d'Otrante (13th century): "The Great Monarch and the Great Pope will precede Antichrist."

"The nations will be in wars for four years and a great part of the world will be destroyed. All the sects will vanish. The capital of the world will fall. The Pope will go over the sea carrying the sign of redemption on his forehead, and after the victory of the Pope and the Great Monarch peace will reign on earth."

"The Pope will cross the sea in a year when the Feast of Saint George (April 23rd) falls on Good Friday, and Saint Mark's feast (April 25th) falls on Easter Sunday, etc." (See Chapter 1, "Questionable Prophecies"; the next year for such a concurrence of feasts is 2038).

"The Great Monarch will come to restore peace and the Pope will share in the victory."

Brother John of the Cleft Rock (1340): "The White Eagle (Great Monarch), by order of the Archangel Michael, will drive the crescent from Europe where none but Christians will remain—he himself will rule from Constantinople. An era of peace and prosperity will begin for the world. There will no longer be Protestants[1] or schismatics; the Lamb will reign and the bliss of the human race will begin. Happy will they be who have escaped the perils of that terrible time, for they can taste of its fruit through the reign of the Holy Ghost and the sanctification of mankind, which can be accomplished only after the defeat of the Black Eagle (Germany).

"God will raise up a holy Pope over whom the angels will rejoice. Enlightened by God, this man will reconstruct almost the entire world through his holiness and lead all to the true faith, and everywhere fear of God, virtue, and good morals will be dominant. He will lead all erring sheep back to the fold, and there shall be only one faith, one law, one rule of life, one baptism on earth. All men will love each other and do good, and all quarrels and war will disappear."

Blessed Joannes Amadeus de Sylva (died 1482): "Germany and Spain will unite under a great prince designated by God. After much slaughtering, the other nations will be forced to come into this union. There is no hope for the unbelievers until all Germany becomes converted; then all will happen quickly. Because of Germany's unfaithfulness, the time will be prolonged until all countries unite under the Great Ruler. After this union, mass conversions will take place by the command of God, and peace and prosperity will follow."

Blessed Catherine of Racconigi (died 1547): "After three centuries a descendant of Francis I of France will rule Europe like Charlemagne."

Telesphorus of Cozensa (died 1388): "A powerful French monarch and French Pope will regain the holy land after terrible wars in Europe, convert the world, and bring universal peace. They will overcome the German Ruler."

David Poreaus (died 1622): "The Great Monarch will be of French descent, large forehead, large dark eyes, light brown wavy hair and an eagle nose. He will crush the enemies of the Pope and will conquer the East."

Holzhauser (died 1658): "When everything has been ruined by war; when Catholics are hard pressed by traitorous co-religionists and heretics; when the Church and her servants are denied their rights, the monarchies have been abolished and their rulers murdered ... then the hand of Almighty God will work a marvelous change, something apparently impossible according to human understanding. There will rise a valiant monarch anointed by God. He will be a Catholic, a descendant of Louis IX, (yet) a descendant of an ancient imperial German family, born in exile. He will rule supreme in temporal matters. The Pope will rule supreme in spiritual matters at the same time. Persecution will cease and justice shall reign. Religion seems to be oppressed, but by the changes of entire kingdoms it will be made more firm.

"He will root out false doctrines and destroy the rule of Moslemism. His dominion will extend from the East to the West. All nations will adore God their Lord according to Catholic teaching. There will be many wise and just men. The people will love justice, and peace will reign over the whole earth, for divine power will bind Satan for many years until the coming of the Son of Perdition.

"The reign of the Great Ruler may be compared with that of Caesar Augustus, who became Emperor after his victory over his enemies, thereby giving peace to the world—also with the reign of Emperor Constantine the Great, who was sent by God, after severe persecutions, to deliver both the Church and State. By his victories on water and land he brought the Roman empire under subjection, which he then ruled in peace . . .

"The Great Monarch will have the special help of God and be unconquerable.

"The Fifth Epoch of time dates from the reign of Charles V until the reign of the Great Monarch.

"The Sixth Epoch from the Great Monarch until Antichrist. This Sixth Epoch of the Church—'the time of consolation'—begins with the Holy Pope and the Powerful Emperor, and terminates with the reign of Antichrist. This will be an age of solace, wherein God will console His Church after the many mortifications and afflictions she had endured in the Fifth period, for all nations will be brought to the unity of the true Catholic Faith."

Rudolph Gekner (died 1675): "A great prince of the North with a most powerful army will traverse all Europe, uproot all republics, and exterminate all rebels. His sword, moved by Divine power, will most valiantly defend the Church of Jesus Christ. He will combat in behalf of the true orthodox faith, and shall subdue to his dominion the Mahometan Empire. A new pastor of the universal church will come from the shore (of Dalmatia) through a celestial prodigy, and in simplicity of heart adorned with the doctrines of Jesus Christ. Peace will be restored to the world."

Monk of Werl (published 1701): "The whole north of Europe will wage war against the whole south led by a strong monarch. This man will restore divine order in the Church, state and family, thus giving true peace to the nations."

Father Lavinsky (died 1708): "The world will be harassed by civil wars and greater destruction than ever before. Germany will be partitioned and have many enemies. Religion will be greatly oppressed and monks will be banished. During their banishment, the Cross, to the astonishment of all, will shine in double splendor through many lands because of the great ruler."

Father Laurence Ricci, S.J. (died 1775): "After the rule of Napoleon a time will come when the people will become poor and the world will be punished in three ways: wars, famines, and pestilences. At a time when the whole world seems doomed, God will intervene. With His aid a valiant duke will arise from the ancient German house which was humiliated by the French monarch. This great ruler will restore stolen Church property. Protestantism will cease and the Turkish empire will end. This duke will be the most powerful monarch on earth. At a gathering of men noted for piety and wisdom he will, with the aid of the Pope, introduce new rules, and ban the spirit of confusion. Everywhere there will be one fold and one shepherd."

Josefa von Bourg (died 1807): "God will choose a descendant of Constantine, Pepin, and St. Louis, who has been tried by a long period of disappointment, to come from exile to rule over Europe. He will have the sign of the cross on his breast and besides being a religious man, will be kind, wise, just and powerful. Under him the Catholic religion will spread as never before."

Abbe Souffrand (died 1828): "The Great Ruler will perform such great and noble deeds that the infidels will be forced to admit the working of God's Providence. Under his reign the greatest righteousness will be practiced and the earth will bear in overabundance.

"Between the cries 'Everything is lost' and 'Everything is saved' there will be scarcely any interval."

Brother Louis Rocco (died 1840): "A Great Monarch will arise after a period of terrible wars and persecutions in

Europe. He will be a Catholic: he will not be German."

Sister Rose Asdenti of Taggia (1847): "A great revolution will spread all over Europe, and peace will not be restored until the white flower, the lily (Bourbon), has taken possession of the throne of France."

Joseph Görres (died 1848): "The people will be united under a powerful monarch who will make new laws and banish corruption from the earth. To the Church will fall the task of rebuilding society. Before this man comes to save them, the people will realize how bitter it is to desert God."

Venerable Magdalene Porzat (died 1850): "An enormous bird (Great Monarch) shall awake as from a sleep, and with its terrible bill and claws shall sever the ox's neck and shall eagerly devour the intestines of the wicked dragon. He shall drag to the mud the tricolor (revolutionary) flag of the French and restore to their dominions the legitimate kings. A just and pious man born in Galicia shall be the Supreme Pontiff; then the whole world shall be united and prosperous. One faith only and one emperor shall reign over the whole earth."

Rev. Theophilus Riesinger, O.M. Cap. (died 1940): "The Great Monarch was destined to have been Archduke Franz Ferdinand (his assassination was the spark that started the first world war), but because of the many 'souls of atonement,' the reign of Antichrist was postponed, and hence also that of the Great Monarch."

*   *   *   *

Reference might also be made here to the prophecies telling of the

Exile and Death of a Pope

Brother John of the Cleft Rock (1340): "Toward the end of the world the Pope with the Cardinals will have to flee Rome under trying circumstances to a place where he will be unknown. He will die a cruel death in this exile. The sufferings of the Church will be much greater than at any previous time in her history."

Bishop George Michael Wittman (died 1833): "Sad days are at hand for the Holy Church of Jesus Christ. The Passion of Jesus will be renewed in the most dolorous manner in the Church and in her Supreme Head . . . Violent hands will be laid on the Supreme Head of the Catholic Church."

Abbess Maria Steiner (died 1862): "Unless people obtain pardon through their prayers, the time will come when they will see the sword and death, and Rome without a shepherd."

Pope Pius IX (died 1878): "The Church will suffer exceedingly. Her servants and her chieftain will be mocked, scourged and martyred."

Pope Saint Pius X (died 1914): "I saw one of my successors by name fleeing over the corpses of his brethren. He will flee to a place for a short respite where he is unknown, but he himself will die a cruel death."

Jacinta of Fatima (died 1920): "I saw the Holy Father in a very big house. He was kneeling before a table holding his face in his hands and he was weeping. Outside there were many people; some were throwing stones, others were cursing at him and saying many ugly words to him."

NOTES

1. There were no Protestants in the 14th century; the word perhaps should be "heretics."

Chapter 6

SPIRITUAL AIDS
IN TIMES OF DISTRESS

The saints, mystics and prophets have told us not only of the chastisements to come, but also how these punishments might be avoided or mitigated, or how we should conduct ourselves if they do fall. This is particularly true of the messages given by Our Lady in approved apparitions in the last century and a half.

Saint Margaret Mary Alacoque (1647-1690): "I understand that devotion to the Sacred Heart is a last effort of His love towards Christians of these latter times, by proposing to them an object and means so calculated to persuade them to love Him."

Father Nectou, S.J. (died 1772): "When those things come to pass which will bring on the triumph of the Church, then will such confusion reign on earth that people will think God has permitted them to have their own contrary will and that the providence of God is not concerned about the world. The confusion will be so general that mankind will not be able to think aright, as if God had entirely withheld His providence from mankind, and during the worst crisis the best that can be done will be to remain where God has placed us, and persevere in fervent prayer."

Mother Maria Rafols (Words of Our Lord—dated 1815, found 1931): "I wish many Communions of reparation.

Also there is the Feast of Christ the King that shall be instituted by My will, and at the proper time, by My beloved son, Pius XI. I wish that it be surrounded with the greatest possible solemnity and splendor. I want My kingdom to be spread throughout the entire world. But in My beloved Spain this Divine fire is to burn with greater intensity, and from there they will carry it throughout the whole world.

"In the times to come there will be many souls who will propagate the devotion to My Divine Heart, and this shall be very agreeable to Me, but those that must do this the most are the sons of My company, for I have chosen them principally for this work so pleasing to Me.

"It is My wish that all men visit the image of My Most Merciful Heart, and to those who devoutly carry it on their person, I promise great graces for eternal salvation.

"All those who wear My medal devoutly shall receive My special protection at the hour of their death.

"<u>Those who wish to obtain the conversion of sinners shall obtain it from My Merciful Heart, by asking it through the mediation of My Most Holy Mother</u>. To all those who seek Me with a lively faith and spirit of prayer, through the intercession of My Most Holy Mother, My Merciful Heart will give Itself. <u>I shall never refuse graces which are asked of Me through the intercession of My Most Holy Mother</u>.

"It is My desire also that the Feast of the Sacred Heart be celebrated throughout the entire Catholic Church with the greatest solemnity, that it be made a holy day of obligation, and that all the faithful receive Holy Communion on that day . . ."

"Therefore the great evil of these times, and of the even worse than these that shall come, always has been and always shall be to lose the memory and taste of the supernatural life, living only for earthly and sinful things.

"When those turbulent and calamitous times will come, the most powerful means to give satisfaction to His Eternal Father will be to invoke His Most Holy Mother under the invocation of *El Pilar,* who is the Patroness and Protectrix of our beloved Spain; and the mental and vocal prayer, meditating on the Five Sorrowful Mysteries of the most holy Rosary, will be the most substantial devotion, and most pleasing to the Virgin of El Pilar, in times of wars, pestilence and persecutions against our most holy religion."

Our Lady to Saint Catherine Labouré (apparitions of 1830): "The times are very evil . . . The entire world will be distressed with afflictions. But do you come to the foot of the altar. There graces will be showered upon all, the great and the small, who ask for them. Graces will be shed most abundantly on those who ask for them."

(After the vision of the Miraculous Medal) "Have a medal struck after this model. All who wear it will receive great graces; they should wear it around the neck. Graces will abound for persons who wear it with confidence."

Blessed Anna Maria Taigi (1769-1837) regarding the Three Days Darkness: "During these three days the people should remain in their homes, pray the Rosary and beg God for mercy."

Our Lady to Saint Bernadette at Lourdes, France (apparitions of 1858): "Penance! Penance! Penance!" "Pray for poor sinners. Pray for the world so troubled."

"Kiss the ground for sinners."

Our Lady at Pontmain, France (1871): "But pray, my children. God will hear you in a short time. My Son allows Himself to be moved by compassion."

Our Lady to Estelle Faguette at Pellevoisin, France (1876): "One can be saved in *every* state. Where you are you can do much good, and you can publish my glory."

"What affects me most is the want of respect shown by some people to my Son in Holy Communion, and the attitude which they assume in prayer when the mind is occupied by other things."

"His Heart has so much love for mine that He cannot refuse my requests. Through me He will move the most hardened hearts. I am come particularly for the conversion of sinners."

"I recommend calm not only for you but also for the Church and France."

"I have chosen thee. I choose the little ones and the weak for my glory."

(In giving the devotion of the Scapular of the Sacred Heart) "The treasures of my Son have been open for a long time, let the people come . . . I love this devotion. It is here I will be honored . . . Nothing will be more acceptable to me than to see this livery on each one of my children, and that they all endeavor to repair the outrages that my Son receives in the Sacrament of His love. See the graces I shall bestow on those who wear it with confidence and who will assist you in propagating it. These graces are from my Son; I took them from His Heart; He can refuse me nothing."

Sister Marie Chambon (died 1907): "The triumph of the Church will be hastened by devotion to the five wounds and the Precious Blood of Jesus Christ."

Fatima (1916) (Prayers taught by the Angel): "My God, I believe, I adore, I hope and I love Thee. I ask pardon for those who do not believe, do not adore, do not hope and do not love Thee."

"Most Holy Trinity, Father, Son and Holy Ghost, I adore Thee profoundly and I offer Thee the most precious Body, Blood, Soul and Divinity of Jesus Christ, present in all the tabernacles of the world, in reparation for the outrages, sacrileges and indifference by which He Himself is offended. And by the infinite merits of His Most Sacred Heart, and the Immaculate Heart of Mary I beg of Thee the conversion of poor sinners."

(Admonitions of the Angel): "Pray! Pray a great deal . . . Offer prayers and sacrifices continually to the Most High . . . Make a sacrifice of everything that you can, and offer it to the Lord as an act of reparation for the sins by which He is offended and of supplication for the conversion of sinners . . . Above all, accept and bear with submission whatever suffering the Lord shall send you."

(1917—Our Lady) "Jesus wishes to establish in the world the devotion to my Immaculate Heart. To those who embrace this devotion He promises salvation. Their souls will be loved by God with a love of predilection, like flowers placed by me before His throne."

"Sacrifice yourselves for sinners, and repeat often, especially whenever you make a sacrifice for them: 'O Jesus, it is for love of Thee, for the conversion of sinners, and in reparation for the sins committed against the Immaculate Heart of Mary.'"

"When you recite the Rosary, say after each mystery: 'O my Jesus, pardon us; save us from the fire of Hell; take all souls to Heaven, especially those in most need.'"

"Pray, pray very much, and make sacrifices for sinners, for many souls go to Hell because they have no one to pray and make sacrifices for them."

"The Rosary must be recited daily. Men must amend their lives and ask pardon for their sins. They must no longer offend Our Divine Lord, who is already too much offended."

(1925) "I promise to assist at the hour of death with the graces necessary for salvation all those who, on the first Saturday of five consecutive months, go to confession, receive Holy Communion, recite the Rosary, and keep me company for a quarter of an hour while meditating on the mysteries of the Rosary, all with the intention of making reparation to me."

Mrs. Marie Mesmin (Nov. 7, 1918): "Do not believe, my children, that now all is ended in this apparent calm. Where are the converted people? Did the world return to God? . . . If the people would do penance, one could say: Soon will come the liberation, the renovation, and a new prosperity in everything. But that is not the case, and dreadful evils await us . . ."

(As revealed by the Mother of God): "By my tears (at La Salette and Bordeaux) I wanted to make you understand that prayer and penance can keep away the punishments . . . If one would pray, nothing would happen. God is powerful enough to govern mankind; all would be renewed in peace without the terrible punishments which will exterminate three fourths of mankind. God does not lack the means whereby to let those disappear who act against His law. If you could obtain a mitigation of the punishment, you would already have attained much."

Pere Lamy (died 1931): "The prayer of the children must be the foundation of everything . . . Prayer offered in union with Our Lady has great power . . . Our Lady requires the sanctity of family life. She requires that disorder should cease and that people should observe order once more. God asks only this so that He may grant them pardon . . . If people had heeded her, the war (1914-1918) would not have come . . . Penance, penance, penance—terrible times are coming. The times we are living in now (1914-1918) are as nothing to what we are soon to see . . . How Our Lord must have suffered! And yet Christians are always seeking pleasure! If it were thus in the green wood, how shall it be in the dry . . . the [First] World War had three causes: blasphemies, work on Sundays, and desecration of marriage . . . Lucifer is playing his last card: he thinks the game is in his hands, in which he is mistaken . . . We must pray confidently in spite of his blustering . . . People will appreciate still more the gentle goodness of Our Blessed Lady . . . Peace will be restored to the world but I shall not see that, and other things will come to pass of which I shall not see the end."

Our Lady at Beauraing, Belgium (1932-1933): "I am the Mother of God and the Queen of Heaven. Pray a great deal. Pray always. I shall convert sinners."

Our Lady at Banneux, Belgium (1933): "I am the Blessed Virgin of the Poor . . . I have come to relieve suffering . . . Believe in me, I shall believe in you . . . Pray a great deal."

Countess Francesca de Billiante (died 1935): "Great tribulations are coming; however, before this, God will send a light of the Church, so that those who follow the light will be given a clear understanding of right and justice. Albertus Magnus will be elevated to the throne of sainthood and recognized as a Doctor of the Church. God will shame the professors of theology with whom He is displeased due to their pride. He will elevate to sainthood the ignorant Brother Konrad and the unknown Brother Jordan Mai. Likewise, God will cause Don Bosco to be canonized. [These things have all come to pass.] In these days the Rosary will bring down untold blessings. We will even know the true Christian by his Rosary."

Priest in Rome (before 1936). According to information from a reliable source, the following prayer was disclosed to a devout priest in Rome during the Holy Sacrifice of the Mass, when it was revealed to him that those who say the prayer with devotion and faith would be spared the great sufferings that were soon to come into the whole world: "O Jesus, Divine Savior! Be merciful. Be merciful to us and to the whole world. Amen. Powerful God! Holy God! Immor-

tal God! Have compassion upon us and upon the whole
world. Amen. Eternal Father, show us mercy, in the name
of the Precious Blood of Thy Only Son, show us mercy we
implore Thee. Amen."

A Bernardine Sister (before 1938) was shown in spirit the
vast devastation caused by the devil throughout the world,
and at the same time heard the Blessed Virgin telling her
that it was true, Hell had been let loose upon the earth, and
that the time had come to pray to her as the Queen of
Angels and to ask of her the assistance of the heavenly
legions to fight against these deadly foes of God and men.
"But, my good Mother," she replied, "you who are so kind,
could you not send them without our asking?" "No," Our
Lady answered, "because prayer is one of the conditions re-
quired by God Himself for obtaining favors." Then the
Blessed Virgin communicated the following prayer, bid-
ding her to have it printed and distributed: "August Queen
of Heaven! Sovereign Mistress of Angels! Thou who from
the beginning has received from God the power and the
mission to crush the head of Satan, we humbly beseech thee
to send thy holy legions, that under thy command, and by
thy power, they may pursue the evil spirits, encounter them
on every side, resist their bold attacks, and drive them
hence into the abyss of eternal woe. Amen."

Sister Faustina (died 1938). About the year 1931 Our Lord
demanded of Sister Faustina the painting of a picture and
indicated to her what it should be like. Unable to paint the
picture herself, she was given permission by the superiors to
instruct an artist in the painting of the picture of the "Mercy
of God." Following are the promises of Our Lord to Sister
Faustina: "I promise that the soul which shall venerate this
picture will not perish. I further promise that soul victory
over its enemies here on earth, and especially in the hour of
death. I Myself shall defend that soul as My own glory . . . I

am giving people a vessel with which they should come to fetch graces from the font of Mercy. That vessel is this picture with the inscription 'Jesus, I trust in Thee.' . . . I desire that the first Sunday after Easter be celebrated as the Feast of Mercy. Anyone who approaches on this day the source of Life will obtain complete remission of sin and punishment. Mankind will not find peace unless it turns with confidence to My Mercy. Before I come as a just judge I will reveal Myself as the King of Mercy so that no one will be able to excuse himself on the Day of Judgment which is slowly approaching."

Our Lady in the Latter Times

Venerable Mary of Agreda (died 1665): "It was revealed to me that through the intercession of the Mother of God all heresies will disappear. This victory over heresies has been reserved by Christ for His Blessed Mother. In the last times the Lord will especially spread the renown of His Mother: Mary began salvation, and by her intercession it will be concluded. Before the Second Coming of Christ, Mary must, more than ever, shine in mercy, might and grace in order to bring unbelievers into the Catholic Faith. The powers of Mary in the last times over the demons will be very conspicuous. Mary will extend the reign of Christ over the heathens and Mohammedans and it will be a time of great joy when Mary, as Mistress and Queen of Hearts, is enthroned."

Saint Louis De Montfort (1673-1716): "The power of Mary over all devils will be particularly outstanding in the last period of time. She will extend the Kingdom of Christ over the idolators and Moslems, and there will come a glorious era in which Mary will be the ruler and Queen of human hearts."

Sister Marie Lataste (died 1847): "Peace shall return to the world because the Blessed Virgin Mary will breathe over the storms and quell them. Her name will be praised, blessed and exalted forever. Prisoners or captives shall recover their liberty; exiles shall return to their country, and the unfortunate or unhappy shall be restored to peace and happiness. Between the most august Mary and her clients there will be a mutual exchange of prayers and graces, of love and affection. From the east to the west, from the north to the south, all shall proclaim the holy name of Mary; Mary conceived without original sin, Mary Queen of Heaven and earth. Amen."

Pope Pius IX (died 1878): "We expect that the Immaculate Virgin and Mother of God, Mary, through her most powerful intercession, will bring it about that our Holy Mother the Catholic Church, after removal of all obstacles and overcoming of all errors, will gain in influence from day to day among all nations and in all places, prosper and rule from ocean to ocean, from the great stream to the ends of the earth; that she will enjoy peace and liberty . . . that all erring souls will return to the path of truth and justice after the darkness of their minds has been dispelled, and that there will be then one fold and one shepherd."

Pope Pius XII (after recommending prayers for peace): "The Virgin Mother of God invoked by such prayers will obtain from the Divine Savior liberation from present anxieties, the peace of hearts and fraternal concord among peoples."

Chapter 7

THE GOSPEL AND THE END OF THE WORLD

Any discussion of the end of the world should begin with the admonition of St. Paul: "We beseech you, brethren, by the coming of Our Lord Jesus Christ and our being gathered together unto Him, not to be hastily shaken from your right mind, nor terrified, whether by spirit, or by utterance, or by letter attributed to us, as though the day of the Lord were near at hand." (2 *Thess.* 2: 1-2).

That the world will come to an end is certain, but *when* it shall come to an end is known to God alone: "But of that day and hour no one knows, not even the angels of heaven, but the Father only." (*Matt.* 24:36).

We have been given certain signs that shall precede Our Lord's coming but it is not certain in what order they shall occur, or how *soon* afterward the end shall come.

The Eschatological Discourse

When in Holy Week Our Lord spoke of the coming destruction of the temple, the apostles came to Him and asked, "Tell us, when are these things to happen, and what will be the sign of Thy coming and of the end of the world?" (*Matt.* 24:3).

The phrasing of the question showed that the apostles perhaps thought the destruction of the temple and the end of the world would occur simultaneously. Our Lord did not correct this misunderstanding because the fall of Jerusalem was to be a *type*[1] of the end of the world, and similar signs would precede each catastrophe. Consequently, in His answer Our Lord first gave several signs that would precede each event, then specific details of both, and concluded, "Amen I say to you, this generation will not pass away till all these things have been accomplished." (*Matt.* 24:34).

This too has a dual interpretation:

(a) Our Lord's generation will see the fall of Jerusalem;

(b) the human race (and the Jewish people) will see the world's end.

Here is the discourse—broken down into topics—as recorded by the evangelists:

False Christs, Wars, Upheavals in Nature

"Take care that no one leads you astray. For many will come in My name, saying, 'I am the Christ,' and they will lead many astray. For you shall hear of wars and rumors of wars. Take care that you do not be alarmed, for these things must come to pass, but the end is not yet. For nation will rise against nation, and kingdom against kingdom; and there will be pestilences and famines and earthquakes in various places. But all these things are the beginnings of sorrow." (*Matt.* 24:4-8).

"Take care that no one leads you astray. For many will come in My name, saying, 'I am he'; and they will lead many astray. But when you hear of wars and rumors of wars, do not be alarmed; for they must come to pass, but the end is not yet. For nation will rise against nation, and kingdom against kingdom; and there will be earthquakes in various places, and famines. These things are the beginning of sorrows." (*Mark* 13:5-8).

"Take care not to be led astray. For many will come in My name, saying, 'I am he,' and, 'The time is at hand.' Do not, therefore, go after them. But when you hear of wars and insurrections do not be terrified; these things must first come to pass, but the end will not be at once." Then He said to them, "Nation will rise against nation, and kingdom against kingdom; and there will be great earthquakes in various places, and pestilences and famines, and there will be terrors and great signs from heaven." (*Luke* 21:8-11).

Persecution

"Then they will deliver you up to tribulation, and will put you to death; and you will be hated by all nations for My name's sake. And then many will fall away, and will betray one another, and will hate one another. And many false prophets will arise, and will lead many astray. And because iniquity will abound, the charity of the many will grow cold. But whoever perseveres to the end, he shall be saved. And this gospel of the kingdom shall be preached in the whole world, for a witness to all nations; and then will come the end." (*Matt.* 24:9-14).

"But be on your guard. For they will deliver you up to councils, and you will be beaten in synagogues, and you will stand before governors and kings for My sake, for a witness to them. And the gospel must first be preached to all nations. And when they lead you away to deliver you up, do not be anxious beforehand what you are to speak; but speak whatever is given you in that hour. For it is not you who are speaking, but the Holy Spirit. And brother will hand over brother to death, and the father his child; children will rise up against parents and put them to death. And you will be hated by all for My name's sake; but he who has persevered to the end will be saved." (*Mark* 13:9-13).

"But before all these things they will arrest you and persecute you, delivering you up to the synagogues and prisons, dragging you before kings and governors for My name's sake. It shall lead to your bearing witness. Resolve therefore in your hearts not to meditate beforehand how you are to make your defense. For I Myself will give you utterance and wisdom, which all your adversaries will not be able to resist or gainsay. But you will be delivered up by your parents and brothers and relatives and friends; and some of you will be put to death and you will be hated by all for My name's sake; yet not a hair of your head shall perish. By your patience you will win your souls." (*Luke* 21:12-19).

Fall of Jerusalem

"Therefore when you see the abomination of desolation, which was spoken of by Daniel the prophet, standing in the holy place—let him who reads understand—then let those who are in Judea flee to the mountains; and let him who is on the housetop not go down to take anything from his house; and let him who is in the field not turn back to take his cloak. But woe to those who are with child, or have infants at the breast in those days! But pray that your flight may not be in the winter, or on the Sabbath. For then there will be great tribulation, such as has not been from the beginning of the world until now, nor will be. And unless those days had been shortened, no living creature would be saved. But for the sake of the elect those days will be shortened." (*Matt.* 24:15-22).

"And when you see the abomination of desolation standing where it ought not—let him who reads understand— then let those who are in Judea flee to the mountains; and let him who is on the housetop not go down and enter to take anything from his house; and let him who is in the field not turn back to take his cloak. But woe to those who are with child, or have infants at the breast in those days! But pray that these things may not happen in winter. For in those days will be tribulations, such as have not been from the beginning of the creation which God created until now, nor will be. And unless the Lord had shortened the days, no living creature would be saved. But for the sake of the elect whom He has chosen, He has shortened the days." (*Mark* 13:14-20).

"And when you see Jerusalem being surrounded by an army, then know that her desolation is at hand. Then let those who are in Judea flee to the mountains; and let those who are in her midst go out, and let those who are in the country not enter her. For these are days of vengeance, that all things that are written may be fulfilled. But woe to those who are with child, or have infants at the breast in those days! For there will be great distress over the land, and wrath upon this people. And they will fall by the edge of the sword, and will be led away as captives to the nations. And Jerusalem will be trodden down by the Gentiles, until the times of the nations be fulfilled." (*Luke* 21:20-24).

The End of the World

"Then if anyone say to you, 'Behold, here is the Christ,' or, 'There he is,' do not believe it. For false christs and false prophets will arise, and will show great signs and wonders, so as to lead astray, if possible, even the elect. Behold, I have told it to you beforehand. If therefore they say to you, 'Behold, he is in the desert,' do not go forth; 'Behold, he is in the inner chambers,' do not believe it. For as the lightning comes forth from the east and shines even in the west, so also will the coming of the Son of Man be. Wherever the body is, there will the eagles be gathered together.

"But immediately after the tribulation of those days, the sun will be darkened, and the moon will not give her light, and the stars will fall from heaven, and the powers of heaven will be shaken. And then will appear the sign of the Son of Man in heaven; and then will all tribes of the earth mourn, and they will see the Son of Man coming upon the clouds of heaven with great power and majesty. And He will send forth His angels with a trumpet and a great sound, and they will gather His elect from the four winds, from one end to the other." (*Matt.* 24: 23-31).

"And then, if anyone say to you, 'Behold, here is the Christ; behold, there he is,' do not believe it. For false christs and false prophets will arise, and will show signs, and wonders, so as to lead astray, if possible, even the elect. Be on your guard, therefore; behold, I have told you all things beforehand.

"But in those days, after that tribulation, the sun will be darkened, and the moon will not give her light, and the stars of heaven will be falling, and the powers that are in heaven will be shaken. And then they will see the Son of Man coming upon clouds with great power and majesty. And then He will send forth His angels, and will gather His elect from the four winds, from the uttermost parts of the earth to the uttermost parts of heaven." (*Mark* 13:21-27).

"And there will be signs in the sun and moon and stars, and upon the earth distress of nations bewildered by the roaring of sea and waves; men fainting for fear and for expectation of the things that are coming on the world; for the powers of heaven will be shaken. And then they will see the Son of Man coming upon a cloud with great power and majesty. But when these things begin to come to pass, look up, and lift up your heads, because your redemption is at hand." (*Luke* 21:25-28).

Conclusion

"Now from the fig tree learn this parable. When its branch is now tender, and the leaves break forth, you know that summer is near. Even so, when you see all these things, know that it is near, even at the door. Amen I say to you, this generation will not pass away till all these things have been accomplished. Heaven[2] and earth will pass away, but My words will not pass away.

"But of that day and hour no one knows, not even the angels of heaven, but the Father only. And as it was in the days of Noe, even so will be the coming of the Son of Man. For as in the days before the flood they were eating and drinking, marrying and giving in marriage until the day Noe entered the ark, and they did not understand until the flood came and swept them all away; even so will be the coming of the Son of Man.

"Then two men will be in the field; one will be taken, and one will be left.[3] Two women will be grinding at the millstone; one will be taken, and one will be left." (*Matt.* 24:32-41).

"Now from the fig tree learn this parable. When its branch is now tender, and the leaves break forth, you know that summer is near. Even so, when you see these things coming to pass, know that it is near, even at the door. Amen I say to you, this generation will not pass away till all these things have been accomplished. Heaven and earth will pass away, but My words will not pass away.

"But of that day or hour no one knows, neither the angels in heaven, nor the Son,[4] but the Father only." (*Mark* 13:28-32).

"Behold the fig tree, and all the trees. When they now put forth their buds, you know that summer is near. Even so, when you see these things coming to pass, know that the kingdom of God is near. Amen I say to you, this generation will not pass away till all things have been accomplished. Heaven and earth will pass away, but My words will not pass away." (*Luke* 21:29-33).

Admonitions

"Watch therefore, for you do not know at what hour your Lord is to come. But of this be assured, that if the householder had known at what hour the thief was coming, he would certainly have watched and not have let his house be broken into. Therefore you also must be ready, because at an hour that you do not expect, the Son of Man will come." (*Matt.* 24:42-44).

"Take heed, watch and pray, for you do not know when the time is: just as a man, when he leaves home to journey abroad, puts his servants in charge, to each his work, and gives orders to the porter to keep watch. Watch, therefore, for you do not know when the master of the house is coming, in the evening, or at midnight, or at cockcrow, or early in the morning; lest coming suddenly he find you sleeping. And what I say to you, I say to all, "Watch."' (*Mark* 13:33-37).

"But take heed to yourselves, lest your hearts be overburdened with self-indulgence and drunkenness and the cares of this life, and that day come upon you suddenly as a snare. For come it will upon all who dwell on the face of all the earth. Watch, then, praying at all times, that you may be accounted worthy to escape all these things that are to be, and to stand before the Son of Man." (*Luke* 21:34-36).

NOTES

1. A biblical person, thing or event which foreshadows and prefigures, by its resemblance, a greater person, thing or event to come. E.g., Moses was a *type* of Christ, Eve was a *type* of Our Lady, and the manna in the desert was a *type* of the Eucharist.
2. Not the abode of the just, but the firmament and all in it.
3. I.e., one will be taken and placed with the saved, the other with the damned.
4. Christ as God knows all things, but the Father did not include the time of the world's end as part of the revelation Christ was to make to mankind.

Chapter 8

SIGNS BEFORE
THE END OF THE WORLD

From the Eschatological Discourse and from other pertinent passages in Scripture, theologians have deduced six signs that must precede the end of the world:

1. Universal preaching of the Gospel.
2. Conversion of the Jews.
3. Return of Henoch and Elias.
4. A great apostasy.
5. The reign of the Antichrist.
6. Extraordinary disturbances in nature.

Universal Preaching of the Gospel

In regard to the first sign, we have Our Lord's words in the Eschatological Discourse: "And this gospel of the kingdom shall be preached in the whole world, for a witness to all nations; and then will come the end." (*Matt.* 24:14).

St. Augustine points out (*Ep.* 199, n. 48) that this does not mean that all men will come into the Church, but simply that the Gospel shall have been preached to all nations and all men given the opportunity to embrace it. He also comments, "What does the phrase 'then it will come' mean except that it will not come before that time. How long after that time it will come we do not know. The only thing we know for certain is that it will not come sooner." (*Ep.* 197,

n. 4) Saint Augustine therefore considers the universal preaching of the Gospel a very remote sign of the world's end.

Conversion of the Jews

Our Lord spoke many times of the light of faith being taken away from the Jews and given to the Gentiles, especially in the parables of the wedding feast and the vinedressers. In foretelling the fall of Jerusalem He concluded, "For there will be great distress over the land, and wrath upon this people. And they will fall by the edge of the sword, and will be led away as captives to the nations. And Jerusalem will be trodden down by the Gentiles, until the times of the nations be fulfilled." (*Luke* 21:23-24). Here there is an allusion that the Jews will not return to their homeland until the light of faith has been offered to "the nations."

There are many Old Testament prophecies which tell of the Jews losing the favor of God and their homeland, and that both will be restored before the end of time:

"For the children of Israel shall sit many days without king, and without prince, without sacrifice, and without altar, and without ephod, and without theraphim. And after this the children of Israel shall return, and shall seek the Lord their God, and David their king: and they shall fear the Lord, and His goodness in the last days." (*Osee* 3:4-5).

"Then shall they cry to the Lord, and He will not hear them: and He will hide His face from them at that time, as they have behaved wickedly in their devices. Thus saith the Lord concerning the prophets that make My people err, that bite with their teeth, and preach peace, and if a man give not something into their mouth, they prepare war against him. Therefore night shall be to you instead of vision, and darkness to you instead of divination; and the sun shall go down upon the prophets, and the day shall be darkened over them. And they shall be confounded that see visions and the diviners shall be confounded; and they shall cover their faces, because there is no answer of God." (*Mich.* 3:4-7).

"Thus saith the Lord of hosts: Behold I will save My people from the land of the east, and from the land of the going down of the sun. And I will bring them, and they shall dwell in the midst of Jerusalem: and they shall be My people, and I will be their God in truth and in justice." (*Zach.* 8:7-8).

"And when Jeremias came hither he found a hollow cave: and he carried in hither the tabernacle, and the ark, and the altar of incense, and so stopped the door. Then some of them that followed him, came up to mark the place: but they could not find it. And when Jeremias perceived it, he blamed them saying: The place shall be unknown, till God gather together the congregation of the people, and receive them to mercy." (2 *Mac.* 2:5-7).

Saint Paul developed this theme: "For I would not, brethren, have you ignorant of this mystery, lest you be wise in your own conceits, that a partial blindness only has befallen Israel, until the full number of the Gentiles should enter, and thus all Israel should be saved, as it is written, 'There will come out of Sion the deliverer and he will take impiety from Jacob; and this is My covenant with them, when I shall take away their sins.'[1] . . . For as you also at one time did not believe God but now have obtained mercy by reason of their unbelief, so they too have not now believed by reason of the mercy shown you, that they too may obtain mercy." (*Romans* 11:25-27, 30-31).

In private revelation we find:

Anne Catherine Emmerich (died 1824): "The Jews shall return to Palestine and become Christians toward the end of the world."

Pope Benedict XV (died 1922): "The return of the Jews to Palestine is the will of God, hence they will have to leave many countries."

Pere Lamy (died 1931): "The Jews are scattered all over the world, but they will not be abandoned. God never forsakes His own."

Return of Henoch and Elias

In the prophecy of Malachias in the Old Testament we read: "Behold I will send you Elias the prophet before the coming of the great and dreadful day of the Lord." (*Mal.* 4:5).

Many of the Jews believed that this prophecy referred to the first coming of the Messiah. This is why the apostles asked Our Lord, "Why then do the Scribes say that Elias must come first?" (*Matt.* 17:10). Our Lord answered, "Elias indeed is to come and will restore all things. But I say to you that Elias has come already, and they did not know him, but did to him whatever they wished ... Then the disciples understood that He had spoken to them of John the Baptist." (*Matt.* 17:11-13).

Thus Saint John the Baptist was the "Elias" whose preaching preceded the first coming of Christ, but Elias himself will appear before the Second Coming.

In regard to Henoch, we find in the book of Ecclesiasticus: "Henoch pleased God, and was translated into paradise that he may give repentance to the nations." (*Ecclus.* 44:16).

In the Apocalypse (11:3-12) mention is made of "two

witnesses" who shall appear before the Second Coming of Christ. From the earliest times it has been believed that these witnesses will be Elias and Henoch preaching repentance to the nations, opposing the Antichrist, and working for the conversion of the Jews.[2]

A Great Apostasy

In his second epistle to the Thessalonians, Saint Paul wrote, "Let no one deceive you in any way, for the day of the Lord will not come unless the apostasy comes first . . ." (2 *Thess.* 2:3).

That great numbers of people shall have become indifferent and shall have fallen away from the Faith is also borne out by the following texts:

"And as it was in the days of Noe, even so will be the coming of the Son of Man. For as in the days before the flood they were eating and drinking, marrying and giving in marriage until the day Noe entered the ark, and they did not understand until the flood came and swept them all away; even so will be the coming of the Son of Man." (*Matt.* 24:37-39).

"Yet when the Son of Man comes, will He find, do you think, faith on the earth?" (*Luke* 18:8).

". . . in the last days there will come deceitful scoffers, men walking according to their own lusts, saying, 'Where is the promise or His coming? For since the fathers fell asleep all things continue as they were from the beginning of creation.'" (2 *Peter* 3:3-4).

NOTES

1. *Isaias* 59:20 and 27:9.
2. According to St. Robert Bellarmine (Doctor of the Church), the return of Henoch and Elias before the Last Judgment is "most true," and he adds that the opposite view is either heretical or approaching heresy. (*Rom. Pont.* 3:6; *De Controv.*)

Chapter 9

THE ANTICHRIST
IN SCRIPTURE

Over and over again in the Eschatological Discourse, Our Lord warned us to beware of false christs. At another time in speaking of the perfidy of the Jews, He said, "I have come in the name of My Father, and you do not receive Me. If another come in his own name, him you will receive." (*John* 5:43). Here is an allusion to a false christ who will be accepted by the Jews.

The term "Antichrist" is found only in the epistles of Saint John. Since the passages are difficult, we will present them parallel *with the interpretations generally given them.*

"Dear children, it is the last hour:
   "the last hour": the last age of the world, the age of the Church;
and as you have heard that Antichrist is coming,
   the early Christians were already familiar with the idea of a personal Antichrist;
so now many antichrists have arisen; whence we know it is the last hour . . ." (1 *John* 2:18).
   "many Antichrists": opponents of Christ; teachers of heretical doctrine.

"He is the Antichrist who denies the Father and the Son." (1 *John* 2:22).
   The *Antichrist will deny God and claim divinity himself (2* Thess. *2:4). However, anyone who*

67

denies God is an Antichrist in himself.

"And every spirit that severs Jesus, is not of God, but is of Antichrist, of whom you have heard that he is coming, and now is already in the world." (1 *John* 4:3).

The heresy of Cerenthus divided Christ into two distinct persons; Saint John places all followers of this heresy in the camp of Antichrist. It is the "spirit" of Antichrist, i.e., the spirit of heresy, that is "already in the world."

"For many deceivers have gone forth into the world who do not confess Jesus as the Christ coming in the flesh. This is the deceiver and the Antichrist." (2 *John* 7).

Again Saint John states that all heretics are in the spirit of the coming Antichrist.

Although the Antichrist is not mentioned by name in any other text in Scripture, there can be no doubt that he is the individual referred to in passages of Daniel, Saint Paul, and the Apocalypse.

In chapters seven through twelve of Daniel, we find long allegorical passages similar in tone and imagery to sections of the Apocalypse.

In chapter seven Daniel beholds in a vision four beasts who are commonly understood to represent the Chaldean, Persian, Grecian and Roman empires. The fourth beast has ten horns, and a variety of interpretations has been given them, such as the ten kingdoms mentioned in Apocalypse 17:12. However, Daniel mentions "another little horn" that sprang out of the ten: "And behold eyes like the eyes of a man were in this horn, and a mouth speaking great things." (*Dan.* 7:8). This is thought to be the Antichrist, though it may also apply to the arch-persecutor of the Jews, Antiochus Epiphanes, who was a type of the Antichrist.

After beholding the kingdom of the Messiah in the same

vision, Daniel returns to the theme of the beasts and the little horn: "I beheld, and lo, that horn made war against the saints, and prevailed over them, till the Ancient of days came and gave judgment to the saints of the Most High, and the time came, and the saints obtained the kingdom.

"And thus He said: 'The fourth beast shall be the fourth kingdom upon earth, which shall be greater than all the kingdoms, and shall devour the whole earth, and shall tread it down, and break it in pieces. And the ten horns of the same kingdom, shall be ten kings. And another shall rise up after them, and he shall be mightier than the former, and he shall bring down three kings. And he shall speak words against the High One, and shall crush the saints of the Most High; and he shall think himself able to change times and laws, and they shall be delivered into his hand until a time, and times, and half a time.[1] And judgment shall sit, that his power may be taken away, and be broken in pieces, and perish even to the end, and that the kingdom, and power, and the greatness of the kingdom, under the whole heaven, may be given to the people of the saints of the Most High, whose kingdom is an everlasting kingdom, and all kings shall serve Him, and obey Him.'" (*Dan.* 7:21-27).

Saint Paul

"Let no one deceive you in any way, for the day of the Lord will not come unless the apostasy comes first, and the man of sin is revealed, the son of perdition, who opposes and is exalted above all that is called God, or that is worshiped, so that he sits in the temple of God and gives himself out as if he were God. Do you not remember that when I was still with you, I used to tell you these things? And now you know what restrains him,[2] that he may be revealed in his proper time. For the mystery of iniquity is already at work; provided only that he who is at present restraining it, does still restrain, until he is gotten out of the way.

"And then the wicked one will be revealed, whom the Lord Jesus will slay with the breath of His mouth and will destroy with the brightness of His coming.

"And his coming is according to the working of Satan[3] with all power and signs and lying wonders, and with all wicked deception to those who are perishing. For they have not received the love of truth that they might be saved. Therefore God sends them a misleading influence that they may believe falsehood, that all may be judged who have not believed the truth, but have preferred wickedness." (2 *Thess.* 2:3-12).

Tribe of Dan

In the seventh chapter of the Apocalypse the tribes of Israel are named, and a certain number in each have the sign of the living God placed on their foreheads. No mention is made of the tribe of Dan. Saint Irenaeus and others believe that this was because the Antichrist would come from that tribe. In support of that theory the following text has been cited:

"Dan shall judge his people like another tribe in Israel. Let Dan be a snake in the way, a serpent in the path, that biteth the horse's heels that his rider may fall backward." (*Genesis* 49:16-17).

NOTES

1. I.e., three and one half years, the length of time Antichrist will reign.
2. The Thessalonians knew what this impediment was, but we do not. Opinions have ranged from the Roman Empire to St. Michael the Archangel.
3. Antichrist will work great prodigies with the aid of Satan.

Chapter 10

THE ANTICHRIST
IN OTHER SOURCES

Early Patristic Writers

Didache (90-100): "In the last days false prophets and corrupters shall be multiplied and the sheep shall be turned into wolves and love into hate. When their iniquity shall have increased they shall hate each other and persecute and betray; and then shall appear the deceiver of the world as the Son of God. And he shall do signs and wonders and the earth shall be given into his hands and he shall do evil such as has not been done through the ages. Then shall all created men come to the fire of judgment and 'many shall be scandalized'[1] and perish.

"He however who shall have persevered in his faith shall be saved from that accursed one. And then shall appear the signs of truth: first the sign of the Heavens opened, secondly the sign of the trumpet, and third the resurrection of the dead; but by no means the resurrection of all, but as is said, 'The Lord shall come and all the saints with Him.'[2] Then the world shall see the Lord coming upon the clouds of Heaven."

Saint Irenaeus (died 200): "By means of the events which shall occur in the time of Antichrist it is shown that he, being an apostate and a robber, is anxious to be adored as God, and that although a mere slave, he wishes himself to be proclaimed as a king. For he, being endued with all the power of the devil, shall come, not as a righteous king, nor as a legitimate king in subjection to God, but an impious, unjust, and lawless one; as an apostate, iniquitous and murderous; as a robber, concentrating in himself satanic apostasy, and setting aside idols to persuade (men) that he himself is God, raising up himself as the only idol, having in himself the multifarious errors of the other idols. This he does in order that they who do worship the devil by means of many abominations may serve himself by this one idol . . ."

Saint Hippolytus (died 235): "For this is what the prophets Henoch and Elias will preach: Believe not the enemy who is to come and be seen; for he is an adversary and corrupter and son of perdition, and deceives you . . ."

Saint Cyprian (died 258): "Nor let any one of you, beloved brethren, be so terrified by the fear of future persecution, or the coming of the threatening Antichrist, as not to be found armed for all things by the evangelical exhortations and precepts, and by the heavenly warnings. Antichrist is coming, but above him comes Christ also. The enemy goeth about and rageth, but immediately the Lord follows to avenge our sufferings and our wounds. The adversary is enraged and threatens, but there is One who can deliver us from his hands.

"For even Antichrist when he shall begin to come, shall not enter the Church because he threatens; neither shall we yield to his arms and violence, because he declares that he will destroy us if we resist. Heretics arm us when they think we are terrified by their threatenings."

Saint Zenobius (died 285): a. "Antichrist, the son of perdition, will be born in Corozain, will be brought up in Bethsaida, and shall begin to reign in Capharnaum, according to what Our Lord Jesus Christ said in the Gospel, 'Woe to thee Corozain . . . Woe to thee Bethsaida . . . and thou Capharnaum, that are exalted up to heaven, thou shalt be thrust down to hell.' (cf. *Luke* 10:13-15).

b. "Antichrist shall work a thousand prodigies on earth. He will make the blind see, the deaf hear, the lame walk, the dead rise,[3] so that even the elect, if possible, shall be deceived by his magical arts. Swollen with pride, Antichrist shall enter in triumph the city of Jerusalem, and will sit on a throne in the temple to be adored as if he were the Son of God. His heart being intoxicated with arrogance, he will forget his being mere man, and the son of a woman of the tribe of Dan. He shall seduce many credulous persons through his deceitful errors . . ."

c. "Elias and Henoch will attack him bodily in the presence of the people, and shall convict him of imposture and lies. Then the Jews of all the tribes of Israel will be converted to the faith of Jesus Christ, and shall suffer martyrdom for His sake. In consequence of this Antichrist shall be seized with rage, and will put to death the two saints of God, and all those who have believed them.

"Then the Son of God, Our Lord Jesus Christ, shall come in person. He shall appear on the clouds of Heaven surrounded by legions of angels and shining with glory. He will put to death Antichrist, the beast, the enemy, the seducer, and all of his followers. This shall be the end of time and the beginning of the general judgment."

Saint Hilary (died 367): "Antichrist will teach that Christ was an imposter and not the real Son of God."

Saint Ephrem (died 375): "When Antichrist begins to rave, the Jews will doubt if he is really the Messiah. He will then remove the Jews from office and treat many of them worse even than the Christians. Antichrist will use worldly goods as bait. He will entice many Christians with money and goods to apostatize. He will give them free land, riches, honor and power. The devil will help him find all the hidden treasures of the world, even those at the bottom of the oceans. With those treasures he will attain greater success for the reign of Satan than at any time in past centuries. The waters will be firm as a rock under his feet and apparently at his command rivers and creeks will change their course so that the water will for a time flow up instead of downstream."

Saint Cyril of Jerusalem (died 386): "Antichrist will exceed in malice, perversity, lust, wickedness, impiety, and heartless cruelty and barbarity all men that have ever disgraced human nature . . . He shall through his great power, deceit and malice, succeed in decoying or forcing to his worship two thirds of mankind; the remaining third part of men will most steadfastly continue true to the faith and worship of Jesus Christ. But in his satanic rage and fury Antichrist will persecute these brave and devout Christians during three years and a half, and torture them with such an extremity of barbarity with all the old and his newly invented instruments of pain, as to exceed all past persecutors of the Church combined. He will oblige all of his followers to bear impressed upon their foreheads or right hands the mark of the beast, and will starve to death all those who refuse to receive it." (cf. *Apoc.* 13:16).

Saint John Chrysostom (died 407): "The world will be faithless and degenerate after the birth of Antichrist."

"Antichrist will be possessed by Satan and be the illegitimate son of a Jewish woman from the East."

Saint Jerome (died 420): "Antichrist will be born near Babylon. He will gain the support of many with gifts and money. He will sell himself to the devil and thereafter will have no guardian angel or conscience."

Saint Benedict (died 543): "During the three and one half years reign of Antichrist, God will send Henoch and Elias to help the Christians."

Medieval Prophecy

Saint John Damascene (died 770): a. "Everybody who denies the Incarnation of the Son of God, and that Jesus Christ is true God and perfect man, such a person is Antichrist. But in a more special and principal manner he will be known as Antichrist who shall come about the end of the world.

b. "His mother will proclaim she gave birth to him while remaining a virgin. He will reign from ocean to ocean.

c. "Antichrist shall be an illegitimate child under the complete power of Satan; and God, knowing his incredible future perversity, will allow the devil to take a full and perpetual possession of him from his very sinful conception.

d. "Though Antichrist will from his childhood have the most wicked and cruel disposition, yet, inspired by a preternatural precocious malice, he will practice the most consummate hypocrisy, deceiving the Jews and all his followers. In proportion as he shall advance in age, knowledge, vice, and power, his ambitions will become excessive . . ."

Rabanus Maurus (died 856): "Antichrist will heal the sick, raise the dead, restore sight to the blind, hearing to the deaf, speech to the dumb, raise storms and calm them, rename mountains, make trees flourish and wither at a word, rebuild the temple of Jerusalem, and make Jerusalem the capital of the world with the vast wealth from hidden treasure."

Saint Methodius (died 885): "In the last period Christians will not appreciate the great grace of God who provided a Great Monarch, a long duration of peace, a splendid fertility of the earth. They will be very ungrateful, lead a sinful life, in pride, in vanity, unchastity, frivolity, hatred, avarice, gluttony, and many other vices so that the sins of men will stink more than a pestilence before God. Many men will doubt whether the Catholic faith is the true and only saving one and whether the Jews are perhaps correct when they still expect the Messias. Many will be the false teachings and resultant bewilderment. The just God will in consequence give Lucifer and all his devils power to come on earth and tempt the godless creatures."

Saint Anselm (died 1109): "Antichrist will rule the world from Jerusalem which he will make into a magnificent city."

Legenda Aurea (12th century): "The Last Judgment will be preceded by the impostor Antichrist, who will try to deceive men in four ways:

   1. By a false exposition of the Scriptures, wherein he will try to prove that he is the Messias promised by the Law.

   2. By accomplishing miracles.

   3. By the distribution of gifts.

   4. By the infliction of punishments."

Blessed Joachim (died 1202): "Toward the end of the world Antichrist will overthrow the Pope and usurp his See."

<u>*Saint Thomas Aquinas*</u> (died 1274): a. "Antichrist will pervert some in his day by exterior persuasion . . . He is the head of all the wicked because in him wickedness is perfect . . . As in Christ dwells the fullness of the Godhead, so in Antichrist the fullness of all wickedness. Not indeed in the sense that his humanity is to be assumed by the devil into unity of person . . . but that the devil by suggestion in-

fuses his wickedness more copiously into him than into all others. In this way all the wicked that have gone before are signs of Antichrist." (*Summa* III, 8:8).

b. "Infidels and even Antichrist are not deprived . . . of the guardianship of angels. Although this help . . . does not result in . . . eternal life by good works, it does none the less . . . protect them from certain evils which would hurt themselves and others. Even the demons are checked by good angels lest they harm as much as they would. In like manner Antichrist will not do as much harm as he would wish." (*Summa* I, 113:4).

c. "As Augustine says, the works of Antichrist may be called lying wonders either because he will deceive men's senses by means of phantoms, so that he will not really do what he seems to do, or because if he works real prodigies they will lead those into falsehood who believe in him." (*Summa* I, 114:4).

d. "His miracles may be said to be real . . . just as Pharaoh's magicians made real frogs . . . but they will not be real miracles because they will be done by the power of natural causes." (*Summa* II II, 178:1).

e. "Although men will be terrified by the signs appearing about the judgment day, yet before those signs begin to appear the wicked will think themselves to be in peace and security after the death of Antichrist and before the coming of Christ, seeing that the world is not at once destroyed as they thought hitherto." (*Summa* Sup., 73:1).

f. "Some say that Henoch and Elias still dwell in that paradise (Eden)." (*Summa* I, 102:2).

g. "Elias was taken up into the atmospheric but not the empyrean heaven, which is the abode of the saints: and likewise Enoch was translated into the earthly paradise, where he is believed to live with Elias until the coming of Antichrist." (*Summa* III, 49:5).

h. "There are two things: the revolt which precedes Antichrist, and the coming of Antichrist. The Faith must first be received in all the world and afterward many are to abandon it. Others speak of a revolt against the Roman Empire to which all the world was subjected, but the nations rejected the empire and Antichrist has not come. Others have it that the Roman Empire did not really cease but merely changed from a temporal into a spiritual kingdom. In this sense the predicted revolt must be against the Catholic Faith of the Roman Church. This is logical enough. Christ came when all were subject to Rome: therefore, a proper sign of the coming of Antichrist is the revolt against Rome.

"As to Antichrist himself, as Christ abounded in a plenitude of virtue, Antichrist will abound in a multitude of all sins, and as Christ is better than all holy persons, so Antichrist is to be worse than all evil men. For this reason he is called the Man of Sin. He is called, too, the Son of Perdition, meaning that he is destined to the extreme of perdition. As all the good and the virtues of the holy ones who preceded Christ were figures of Christ, so in all the persecutions of the Church the tyrants were and shall be figures of Antichrist, and all the malice which lay hidden in them will be revealed at that time.

i. "The crime of Antichrist is duplex: He is against God and he puts himself above Christ. In opposing God, he puts himself above the true God, in place of all false gods, and even denies the participation of humans in the Godhead. The pride of Antichrist surpasses that of all his predecessors, and like Caesar and the King of Tyre he will say he is God and man, and so represented he will sit in the temple.

j. "Some say that Antichrist is of the tribe of Dan and that, therefore, the Jews will first receive him and will rebuild the temple of Jerusalem, and it will be in this temple that he will sit. Others, however, maintain that never will Jerusalem or the temple be rebuilt, and that he will sit in the Church in the sense that many from the Church will receive him. St. Augustine says that he with his adherents will form a church just as Christ and His followers are a Church.

k. "Antichrist will come in God's good time. Those who now work evil, pretending it is good, do the work of Antichrist. The devil, in whose power Antichrist comes, already in the time of Saint Paul was working his iniquity in a hidden manner through tyrants and seducers because the persecutions of times past are figures of that ultimate persecution against all good persons and are imperfect when compared to it.

l. "Antichrist will be destroyed by the spirit of the mouth of Christ, that is, by the Holy Ghost or by Christ's command in that Michael will kill him on Mt. Olivet whence Christ ascended into Heaven, just as Julian (the Apostate) was extinguished by the divine hand.

m. "Antichrist will enjoy the use of free will on which the devil will operate, as it was said of Judas: 'Satan entered into him,' that is, by instigating him. He shall deceive both by worldly power and the operation of miracles. In the matter of worldly power, Saint John (*Apoc.* 13) says, 'He will control the treasures of gold and silver and all the precious things of Egypt.' The power of miracles will be simulated. 'He will do wondrous signs and even make fire come upon the earth' (*Daniel* 11) and thus, he will 'lead many into error, even, were it possible, the elect.' (*Matt.* 24).

n. "But his miracles will be lies. No one can perform a true miracle against the Faith, because God is not a witness of falsity. Hence, no one preaching a false doctrine can work miracles, whereas one leading a bad life could." (*Comment. in II Thess. II,* Lec. 1-3).

Saint Mechtilda (died 1299): "Henoch and Elias will expose the devilish trickery of Antichrist to the people. As a consequence he will put them to death. For three and one half days their bodies will be exposed to insults, and the followers of Antichrist will presume that all danger is now past, but suddenly the bodies of the two prophets will move, rise and gaze on the crowd and begin to praise God. A great earthquake similar to that at Christ's resurrection will take place: Jerusalem will be partially destroyed and thousands killed. Then a voice from Heaven will call out, 'Ascend!' whereupon the prophets will ascend into Heaven, resulting in the conversion of many. Antichrist will reign thirty days after their ascension."

Richard Rolle of Hampole (died 1349): "After the destruction of Rome, Antichrist will appear and exalt himself above pagan deities and the Trinity. His name signifies one who is against Christ. Begotten of a sinful man and a woman into whom the devil has entered, Antichrist will be born of the tribe of Dan in the city of Corozain. The good angel assigned to him at his birth will be obliged to leave him as witches, necromancers and other disreputable characters will take charge of his education in Bethsaida. Coming to Jerusalem, he will proclaim himself Christ and at first feign to be holy. He will succeed through false preaching, miracles, gifts, terror, aided throughout by the devil. An evil spirit will come out of the air and descend upon his followers. He shall feign a resurrection from the dead, cause rain to fall, stone images to speak, and perform other wonders, all through the power of the devil. The recalling of the dead to life will be only apparent; devils entering the dead bodies will cause the illusion. Antichrist will be the greatest tyrant of all time. His adherents will be marked with his sign. Devils shall be let loose from Hell. The Jews will welcome him."

Saint Vincent Ferrer (died 1418): "In the days of peace that are to come after the desolation of revolutions and wars, before the end of the world, the Christians will become so lax in their religion that they will refuse to receive the Sacrament of Confirmation, saying, 'It is an unnecessary Sacrament'; and when the false prophet, the precursor of

Antichrist, comes, all who are not confirmed will apostatize, while those who are confirmed will stand firm in the Faith, and only a few will renounce Christ."

Modern Prophecy

Francisco Suarez (died 1617). Suarez (following Saint Jerome, Saint Ambrose, Sulpitius Severus, *et al.*) says that "Antichrist shall be born of Jewish extraction, and will profess the Jewish religion, not through real devotion, but through hypocrisy, in order more easily to persuade the great majority of that mysterious race to receive him as their Messiah. He will have two important objects in doing this. In the first place he will thus mimic Jesus Christ; in the second place, he will thus obtain the enthusiastic support and the wealth of the Jews, and through this material advantage be able to open the way to his ambition for high dignities and human power . . . Our Divine Lord and Savior Jesus Christ was born from the Jewish race, and preaching to them the truth, confirmed it with many incontestable miracles, yet they obstinately refused to believe in Him or in His doctrines. Antichrist shall be born from the same people, who will allow themselves to be deceived by his satanic power, signs, and lying wonders, and will enthusiastically receive him as their long-expected Messiah. Thus we see how obstinacy in error leads men to greater crimes and to final reprobation. Because they receive not the love of truth, that they may be saved; therefore God sent them the operation of error to believe a lie."

The Sibylle, Queen Michaula of Saba (printed 1619): "As Henoch and Elias will preach against the Antichrist and draw many away from him, he will, as soon as he perceives the damage, march toward Jerusalem in order to prove there that he is the true Messiah and God. He will kill both prophets in Jerusalem. Their bodies will remain lying in the streets unburied, but on the fourth day they will be resurrected by a voice from Heaven, 'Henoch and Elias arise!' and rise to Heaven in a cloud. Then the followers of Antichrist will regret having believed him and will repent of their sins. Thereupon Antichrist will make it known that after fifteen days he also will ascend into Heaven, so that no one can doubt his divinity. On the appointed day he will majestically seat himself on a beautiful chair, on Mt. Olivet, in view of a large crowd, and before all the people will lift himself up toward Heaven through the help of the devil. But, here at the command of God, the Archangel Michael will cast him down to earth by a stroke of lightning."

Venerable Bartholomew Holzhauser (died 1658): "Antichrist will come as the Messiah from a land between two seas in the East.

"He will be born in the desert, his mother being a prostitute to the Jews and Hindus. He will be a lying and false prophet and will try to rise to Heaven like Elias.

"He will begin work in the East, as a soldier and preacher of religion when thirty years old.

"Antichrist and his army will conquer Rome, kill the Pope and take the throne.

"He will restore the Turkish regime destroyed by the Great Monarch. The Jews, knowing from the Bible that Jerusalem will be the seat of the Messiah, will come from everywhere, and accept Antichrist as the Messiah.

"He will be able to fly. His flight will take place from Mt. Calvary. He will tell the crowd he is going after Henoch and Elias (who had arisen from the dead) in order to kill them again.

"Antichrist will live fifty five and one half years, that is, 666 months."

Venerable Maria of Agreda (died 1665): "When the world

will be drowned in terrible vices, Satan and all his devils will be let loose so that they may pave the way for the godless Antichrist to attain world dominion and final persecution.

"As mankind has lost its faith, the subjects of that time will be very much oppressed by their rulers and authorities. Then many people will come to the Antichrist, who will pretend to be exceedingly kind and generous to all, and tell him their troubles. He will console the oppressed and promise them help. Finally the delegates of certain nations, the Jews, Turks and Tartars will beg him to personally free them from their unbearable yoke. He will now declare himself ready to fulfill their wishes, while at the same time he will arouse the neighboring nations to revolution. The Jews will finally bring him a costly crown and a kingly garment, as well as a scepter, and declare him their freely elected king. The kings of the world, who will hear of this, will laugh at it and not pay any attention to this little horn. In the meantime he will build a powerful army and take up residence in Babylon, where a magnificent palace will be built for him. Many Jews will then stream to Babylon. Then the Antichrist will seek to enlarge his kingdom. He will, therefore, occupy with his troops various surrounding districts in Asia. Then, like a storm wind, he will appear in Egypt with his army and conquer this country as well as Ethiopia. He will then endeavor to make himself loved by the subjugated nations by a friendly behavior, and by exacting a very small tribute from them. He will declare everywhere that he is destined to be the Savior of all the oppressed. He will not in the least let it be known that he strives for a world kingdom. Thereupon he will march into the promised land and occupy Jerusalem. Now, at last, the kings of the world will become frightened; they will recognize that they are dealing with the Antichrist, especially since the Jews of the whole world will make known the great talents and deeds of the Antichrist, so that his praise shall resound throughout the world. Then the kings will send armies to the Holy Land, but the Antichrist will slay them all."

Dionysius of Luxemberg (died 1682): a. "After the birth of Antichrist the people of the world will be very wicked and godless. People of real virtue will be very scarce. Pastors in many places will neglect the service of God, and will live with women. Even the relgous will crave for worldly things. The churches will be dreary and empty like deserted barns . . . At the time when Antichrist is about twenty years of age the whole world will be without faith, subjects will be oppressed by rulers and others in authority. In every period of tribulation God aids His Church, and He will do it in the time before the coming of Antichrist. From the midst of His Church He will raise up a Christian ruler who will perform most remarkable deeds. With divine assistance this ruler will not only lead erring souls back to the true Faith but also deal a heavy blow to the foes of the empire, the Turks, to take away their empire and restore it to Christianity.

b. "The conception of Antichrist will be like Christ's except it will be by the devil[4] instead of the Holy Ghost. He will have the devil's power like Christ had God's.

c. "Antichrist will present himself to the Jews as the Messiah. They will be his first followers.

d. "Antichrist will have the powers of the devil from the beginning. He will be so evil it would seem his father was the devil. He will inherit his evil tendencies from his mother, who will also train him in evil.

e. "His wife will be a Jewess but he will have many women, especially the daughters of rulers.

f. "Antichrist's life will be a mockery of Christ's. He will be a convincing speaker, have great knowledge, the gift of tongues, and be a child wonder at six or seven.

g. "He will take the riches of the world to Jerusalem and appear to have power over natural laws.

h. "Antichrist will be an iconoclast (even against pagan images). Most of the world will adore him. He will teach that the Christian religion is false, confiscation of Christian property is legal, Saturday is to be observed instead of Sunday, and he will change the ten commandments. All his wonders could not be written in a book. They will be more wonderful than the Old and New Testaments. All with the mark of Antichrist will be possessed by the devil. There will be persecution without rest for those who do not have the mark. He will read people's minds, raise the dead, reward his followers and punish the rest.

i. "Elias will cause the rain, dew and snow to cease in those countries where the inhabitants oppose the two prophets and refuse to reject Antichrist. The first land to be so punished will be Palestine in order to win over the Jews.

j. "After Elias finds the Ark of the Covenant of the Jews (2 *Mac.* 2:5-7) he and Henoch will place the Blessed Sacrament upon it. The Jews will then realize that Jesus Christ and not Antichrist is the true Messiah. They will desert Antichrist and make a pilgrimage to Mount Nebo (where the Ark is found) bewailing the hardheartedness of their ancestors. Thereafter they will accept the Christian faith.

k. "The Antichrist will kill Henoch and Elias and leave them unburied. These will, however, be resurrected after three and one half days and ascend into Heaven in a cloud in the presence of their enemy. This miraculous event will actually confuse Antichrist. In order that the nations will not abandon him, he will lift himself up with great majesty into space on Mt. Olivet, with the purported intention to cast down the prophets who have ascended into Heaven. But, in this moment Christ will strike him down. The earth will open and swallow him and his prophets alive. Then a large part of Jerusalem will fall into ruins from the earthquake."

Anne Catherine Emmerich (died 1824): a. "In the center of

Hell I saw a dark and horrible-looking abyss, and into this Lucifer was cast, after being first strongly secured with chains; thick clouds of sulphurous black smoke arose from its fearful depths and enveloped his fearful form in the dismal folds, thus effectually concealing him from every beholder. God Himself had decreed this: and I was likewise told, if I remember right, that he will be unchained for a time fifty or sixty years before the year of Christ 2000. The dates of many other events were pointed out to me which I do not now remember, but a certain number of demons are to be let loose much earlier than Lucifer, in order to tempt men, and to serve as instruments of the divine vengeance.

b. "Antichrist will fight a successful battle at Mageddo in Palestine after which seven rulers, from fear, will subject themselves to Antichrist and he will thereafter become lord of the world.

c. "I see new martyrs, not of the present time, but in the next century. I see them pursued. I see how here and there good and pious people, and especially the religious orders, are tortured, imprisoned and murdered . . .

d. "I saw a picture of a dreadful battle. The entire field was covered with vapors. They shot everywhere out of thickets, which were full of soldiers, and out of the air. The place was low-lying territory and in the distance were great cities. I saw Saint Michael descending with a great multitude of angels and dispersing the combatants. That, however, will happen when everything seems lost. There will be a leader who will invoke Saint Michael and then victory will descend. The enemy were in the majority but the small loyal band overthrew whole lines. It was a frightful battle, and at last only a small band of good people were left and they became the victor.

e. "I wish the time were here when the Pope dressed in red will reign. I see the Apostles, not those of the past, but the apostles of the last times, and it seems to me the Pope is among them."

Rev. Frederick William Faber (died 1863): a. "From the first, all the troubles of the Church were regarded as types of Antichrist, as Christ had His types; so we naturally conclude with this. It is not an idle speculation; Scripture puts it before us.

b. The person of Antichrist.

1. A single person. 'The man of sin, the son of perdition, that wicked one.' (2 *Thess.* 2:3). 'This is Antichrist, who denieth the Father and the Son.' (1 *John* 2:22).

2. Many believe in a demoniacal incarnation—this will not be so—but he will be a man utterly possessed. (*Cardinal Berulle*).

3. Not yet come—Mahomet was not he—the signs are not fulfilled.

4. He is to be a king—his kingdom in visible antagonism to the kingdom of Christ—so all civil oppositions have been precursors of Antichrist.

5. Certainly a Jew—uncertain if of the tribe of Dan—origin probably obscure.

6. With zeal for the temple, gives himself out as the Messiah.

7. With immense talents, awfully assisted by the devil—immense wealth—immoral—unparalleled in deceit, deceiving even the elect.

8. His doctrine an apparent contradiction of no religion, yet a new religion. Comparison with the French Revolution: (1) He denies the divinity of Christ. (2) Asserts that he is the Messias. (3) Worship of devils. (4) He is an atheist, (5) but begins by affecting respect for the law of Moses. (6) Lying miracles, false resurrection, mock ascension. (7) He has an attendant pontiff, so separating regal and prophetic office.

c. His kingdom.

1. Not hereditary—got by decrees, by fraud, talent and

iniquitous diplomacy.

2. It will begin at Babylon. (*Zach.* 5:11).

3. It will extend in influence over the whole civilized world.

4. Jerusalem will be the metropolis.

5. When his empire is at its full, it will last only three years and a half.

  d. His persecution.

    1. Unparalleled horror of it. (*Apoc.* 20).

    2. In spiritual things: (1) there will be hardly any Mass, (2) but the worship of his image and the wearing of his mark; (3) majority of Christians will apostatize, (4) but the Church will not be destroyed.

    3. Saints will be greater than ever—martyrs greater: as the first fought against men, the latter will fight against devils.

    4. Henoch and Elias, now confirmed in grace and waiting; they will preach in sackcloth for as long a time as Christ, i.e., three years and a half less nineteen days. Their martyrdom—they will lie unburied.

    5. Jesus kills him, and the doom comes forty-five days after; some say that St. Michael will kill him on Mount Olivet.

  e. Protestantism an anticipation of Antichrist.

    1. Its attitude toward the Blessed Virgin Mary, the Mass, the sign of the cross.

    2. All its sects unite against the Church.

    3. Its carelessness about Baptism.

    4. It blasphemes saints.

  f. The five-and-forty days.

    1. Space for repentance.

    2. Full of signs.

    3. The Lord comes and the weary world is judged and burned.

  g. Lessons.

    1. The reign of Antichrist is to be the last temporal

reign: so the Church's last enemy is to be a kingdom, the consummation of the wickedness of all kingdoms. How significant!

2. What part should we take in this persecution? Let us measure it by the boldness of our professions now—by our strictness with ourselves—by our self-denial in charity for others—by our perseverance in the practices of penance—by the fervor and the frequency of our prayers—by the rigorousness of the examination of our conscience. It is always for each of us the five-and-forty days. Christ will come—He will not tarry—let us have our loins girded and our lamps burning, that when the midnight cry is raised and the Bridegroom cometh, we may go forward with holy awe to meet our Savior and our Judge."

Summation

It will be noted that many of the preceding prophecies agree on several points concerning the Antichrist: his coming from the East, of the tribe of Dan, born of a Jewish mother; his prodigies; his enthronement in Jerusalem; his being accepted as the Messiah by the Jews; his being opposed by Henoch and Elias, and his murder of these prophets. There *is* disagreement on what follows. Saint Zenobius prophesies that Christ will appear in the clouds immediately following the death of Henoch and Elias and will Himself put the Antichrist to death.

Saint Mechtilda foretells the resurrection and ascension of the two prophets three and a half days after their death, and that "Antichrist will reign thirty days after the ascension."

The Sibylle, Queen Michaula of Saba, prophesies the death of Antichrist (by Saint Michael) *fifteen* days after the ascension of the prophets, when Antichrist will attempt a false ascension. The same prophecy is made by Dionysius of Luxemberg but he does not specify the time between the true and false ascensions.

Father Faber allows forty-five days between the death of Antichrist and the Second Coming of Our Lord.

Saint Thomas tells only of an indefinite period: "The wicked will think themselves to be in peace and security after the death of Antichrist and before the coming of Christ, seeing that the world is not at once destroyed as they thought hitherto."

Some of these prophecies may have been intended more as opinions, or commentaries on Scriptural passages, especially chapter eleven of the Apocalypse. Those who foretold the Antichrist raising the dead to life may have meant to express the idea that he will *seem* to raise the dead to life, in the manner explained by Richard Rolle of Hampole.

In recent years a private paper on the Earling possession case has been widely circulated. According to its contents the Antichrist was to reign from 1952 to 1955; the Great Monarch opposing him was to be Otto of Hapsburg; the three days darkness was to come in 1955, terminating the reign of Antichrist. None of these events took place as prophesied, showing the paper to be worthless.

NOTES

1. I.e., led into evil-doing.
2. *Zach.* 14:5. The author of the *Didache* either did not expect the resurrection of the damned, or was here thinking of the Millenium.
3. This is denied by St. Thomas and others. See Richard Rolle of Hampole (page 80). Appendix C, however, describes an African resurrection ceremony.
4. This is denied by St. Thomas and others. The meaning, as shown in "d" of the same prophecy, is perhaps that his father will be a notoriously wicked man, moved by the devil.

Chapter 11

EXTRAORDINARY DISTURBANCES IN NATURE

The sixth sign of the end of the world will be extraordinary disturbances in nature. These might be divided into two classes: those that will *precede* the world's end, and those that will *accompany* it.

In the first group we might include the following texts:

". . . and there will be pestilences and famines and earthquakes in various places." (*Matt.* 24:7).

". . . and there will be earthquakes in various places, and famines." (*Mark* 13:8).

". . . and there will be great earthquakes in various places, and pestilences and famines, and there will be terrors and great signs from heaven." (*Luke* 21:11).

And in the second group:

"Behold, the day of the Lord shall come, a cruel day, and full of indignation, and of wrath, and fury, to lay the land desolate, and to destroy the sinners thereof out of it. For the stars of heaven, and their brightness shall not display their light; the sun shall be darkened in his rising, and the moon shall not shine with her light." (*Isaias* 13:9-10).

". . . the day of the Lord is near in the valley of destruction. The sun and the moon are darkened, and the stars have withdrawn their shining. And the Lord shall roar out of Sion, and utter His voice from Jerusalem; and the heavens and earth shall be moved . . ." (*Joel* 3:14-16).

". . . the sun will be darkened, and the moon will not give her light, and the stars will fall from heaven, and the powers of heaven will be shaken." (*Matt.* 24:29).

". . . the sun will be darkened, and the moon will not give her light, and the stars of heaven will be falling, and the powers that are in heaven will be shaken." (*Mark* 13:24-25).

"And there will be signs in the sun and moon and stars, and upon the earth distress of nations bewildered by the roaring of sea and waves; men fainting for fear and expectation of the things that are coming on the world; for the powers of heaven will be shaken." (*Luke* 21:25-26).

Private revelation adds a note about Ireland:

Attributed to Saint Patrick (died 493): "The ocean shall inundate Ireland seven years before the end so that the devil may not rule over that people."

Saint Columbkille (died 597): "Seven years before the last day the sea shall submerge Ireland in one inundation."

Saint Nennius: "The sea will come over Ireland seven years before the Day of Judgment."

Leabhar Breac: "The sea shall overwhelm Ireland seven years before the Judgment."

John O'Connell (died 1858): "Lest the deceptions, snares,

and danger of Antichrist should fall upon the Irish, He promised to send a deluge over Ireland, seven years previous to the burning of the spheres."

These private prophecies should not be taken seriously. If Ireland were to disappear in the sea, mankind would then know for certain the end of the world was only seven years away.

Chapter 12

THE APOCALYPSE

The Apocalypse, the sole prophetic book of the New Testament, was written by Saint John the Apostle on the island of Patmos around the year 96 A.D.

It is thought that just as the book of Daniel was written to comfort the Jews under the cruel persecution of Antiochus Epiphanes, so the Apocalypse was written to sustain the early Christians in the persecution under Domitian.

Some commentators understand the prophecy as pertaining almost wholly to Saint John's day. Others hold that it is concerned chiefly with the last days. A third group sees it as a great allegory (and there is no time sequence in an allegory) depicting the constant struggle between the forces of Good and Evil, with special application to the time of Saint John, of the Antichrist, and the end of the world.

On the side of Good appear God, Our Lord in His human and divine natures (and in imagery as "the Lamb who was slain"), Saint Michael and the faithful angels, all the saints, the Church Militant on earth and the Two Witnesses.

Opposing them on the side of Evil are Satan (under several guises), the fallen angels, pagan Rome and the pagan priesthood, all persecutors of the Church, the Antichrist and his followers.

The souls of men are the prize in this struggle, and the prophecy tells of the complete, final triumph of the forces of Good.

As in the Eschatological Discourse the fall of Jerusalem was given as a type of the end of the world, so in the

Apocalypse Nero and Domitian appear as forerunners of the Antichrist, and pagan Rome as a type of the Antichrist's kingdom.

Contents

The Apocalypse opens with a declaration of its theme and purpose, and the identification of its author:

"The revelation of Jesus Christ which God gave Him, to make known to His servants the things that must shortly come to pass; and He sent and signified them through His angel to His servant John; who bore witness to the word of God and to the testimony of Jesus Christ, to whatever he saw. Blessed is he who reads and those who hear the words of this prophecy, and keep the things that are written therein; for the time is at hand." (1:3).

Letters are then written to the "angels" (i.e., bishops) of the seven churches in Asia Minor, discussing their problems and shortcomings, and prescribing remedies with many exhortations. (1:4-3:22).

The Seven Seals (4:1-8:5)

The prophecy proper begins in chapter four with a vision of the court of Heaven, and the opening of the book with the seven seals by "the Lamb who was slain."

At the breaking of the first four seals the Four Horsemen of the Apocalypse appear: Conquest, War, Famine and Death:

"And power was given them over a fourth part of the earth" (6:8 translated from the Greek by Bishop Challoner).

When the fifth seal is broken, the martyrs ask for retribution for the shedding of their blood, and each is given a white garment.

Prodigies follow the breaking of the sixth seal: a great earthquake and signs in the sun, moon and stars. Terror strikes the peoples of the earth, and they try to hide from the wrath to come. Four angels appear holding four winds, but they are restrained from releasing them until the servants of God receive the seal of the living God on their foreheads. <u>One hundred forty-four thousand persons of the tribes of Israel are signed with this seal</u>. Saint John then sees the following:

". . . a great multitude which no man could number, out of all nations and tribes and peoples and tongues, standing before the throne and before the Lamb, clothed in white robes, and with palms in their hands. And they cried with a loud voice, saying, 'Salvation belongs to our God who sits upon the throne, and to the Lamb.'. . . These are they who have come out of the great tribulation, and have washed their robes and made them white in the blood of the Lamb. Therefore they are before the throne of God, and serve Him day and night in His temple, and He who sits upon the throne will dwell with them. They shall neither hunger nor thirst any more, neither shall the sun strike them nor any heat. For the Lamb who is in the midst of the throne will shepherd them, and guide them to the fountains of the waters of life, and God will wipe away every tear from their eyes." (7:9-10, 14-17).

At the breaking of the seventh seal, seven angels appear and each is given a trumpet.

The Seven Trumpets (8:6-11:19)

At the sound of the first four trumpets the following catastrophes occur:

(a) hail and fire mingled with blood are cast upon the

earth, burning up a third part of the earth, the trees and the grass;

(b) a burning mountain is cast into the sea, turning a third of the water into blood, killing a third of the creatures in the sea, and destroying a third of the ships;

(c) a burning star falls upon the third part of the rivers and fountains, turning them into wormwood, causing the death of many people because of the bitterness of the waters;

(d) the sun, moon and stars lose the third part of their intensity of light.

At the sound of the fifth trumpet, a star (thought to be Lucifer) falls from Heaven to earth, and he is given the key to the bottomless pit (i.e., Hell). He opens the pit, and the sun and air are darkened by the smoke that comes forth. Locusts and scorpions emerge and are given permission to torture mankind for five months, but they have no power to injure those who are sealed with the sign of the living God.

When the sixth trumpet sounds, the four angels bound at the river Euphrates are loosed "that they might kill the third part of mankind." (9:15). They are followed by horsemen ("twenty thousand times ten thousand"), and from the mouths of the horses issue forth fire, smoke and sulphur by which the third part of mankind is wiped out.

Mankind, seeing these plagues, is still unconverted and perseveres in evil.

An angel of magnificent appearance descends from Heaven, "clothed in a cloud, and the rainbow was over his head, and his face was like the sun, and his feet like pillars of fire." (10:1). He gives John a scroll to eat, and says that the mystery of God shall be accomplished with the sounding of the seventh trumpet.

John is given a reed to measure the temple and is told that the holy city will be trampled underfoot for forty-two months—the first mention in the Apocalypse of the three and one half years mentioned by Daniel, the length of the

Antichrist's reign.

The Two Witnesses are introduced and they prophesy for "a thousand two hundred and sixty days" (11:3)—the second mention of the three and one half years. When they have finished their testimony they are slain by the beast. (11:7). (This is the first appearance of the beast, thought to represent Antichrist.) Their bodies remain exposed for three and one half days while the inhabitants of the earth make merry over them. They are then restored to life and ascend to Heaven on a cloud. A great earthquake strikes Jerusalem, killing seven thousand people and destroying the tenth part of the city. The remaining inhabitants are converted.

The seventh trumpet is sounded: a song of praise is heard and the temple of God in Heaven is opened, accompanied by flashes of lightning, peals of thunder, an earthquake and great hail.

The Divine Drama (12:1-18)

"And a great sign appeared in heaven: a woman[1] clothed with the sun, and the moon was under her feet, and upon her head a crown of twelve stars. And being with child, she cried out in her travail and was in the anguish of delivery. And another sign was seen in heaven, and behold, a great red dragon having seven heads and ten horns, and upon his heads seven diadems. And his tail was dragging along the third part of the stars of heaven,[2] and it dashed them to the earth; and the dragon stood before the woman who was about to bring forth, that when she had brought forth he might devour her son. And she brought forth a male child, who is to rule all nations with a rod of iron; and her child was caught up to God and to His throne. And the woman fled into the wilderness, where she has a place prepared by God, that there they may nourish her a thousand two hundred and sixty days.[3]

"And there was a battle in heaven;[4] Michael and his angels battled with the dragon, and the dragon fought and his angels. And they did not prevail, neither was their place found any more in heaven. And that great dragon was cast down, the ancient serpent, he who is called the devil and Satan, who leads astray the whole world; and he was cast down to the earth and with him his angels were cast down." (12:1-9).

After a song of triumph celebrating Satan's overthrow, the drama continues:

"And when the dragon saw that he was cast down to the earth, he pursued the woman who had brought forth the male child. And there were given to the woman the two wings of the great eagle, that she might fly into the wilderness unto her place, where she is nourished for a time and times and a half time,[5] away from the serpent. And the serpent cast out of his mouth after the woman water like a river, that he might cause her to be carried away by the river. And the earth helped the woman, and the earth opened her mouth and swallowed up the river that the dragon had cast out of his mouth. And the dragon was angered at the woman, and went away to wage war with the rest of her offspring,[6] who keep the commandments of God, and hold fast the testimony of Jesus. And he stood upon the sand of the sea." (12:13-18).

The Two Beasts (13:1-18)

"And I saw a beast[7] coming up out of the sea, having seven heads and ten horns, and upon its horns ten diadems, and upon its heads blasphemous names. And the beast that I saw was like a leopard, and its feet were like the feet of a bear, and its mouth like the mouth of a lion. And the dragon gave it his own might and great authority. And one of its heads was smitten, as it were, unto death; but its deadly wound was healed. And all the earth followed the beast in wonder. And they worshiped the dragon because he gave authority to the beast, and they worshiped the beast, saying, 'Who is like to the beast, and who will be able to fight with it?'

"And there was given to it a mouth speaking great things and blasphemies; and there was given to it authority to work for forty-two months.[8] And it opened its mouth for blasphemies against God, to blaspheme His name and His tabernacle, and those who dwell in heaven. And it was allowed to wage war with the saints and to overcome them. And there was given to it authority over every tribe, and people, and tongue, and nation. And all the inhabitants of the earth will worship it whose names have not been written in the book of life of the Lamb who has been slain from the foundation of the world.

"If any man has an ear, let him hear. He who is for captivity, into captivity he goes; he who kills by the sword, by the sword must he be killed. Here is the patience and the faith of the saints.[9]

"And I saw another beast[10] coming up out of the earth, and it had two horns like to those of a lamb, but it spoke as does a dragon. And it exercised all the authority of the former beast in its sight; and it made the earth and the inhabitants therein to worship the first beast, whose deadly wound was healed. And it did great signs, so as even to make fire come down from heaven upon earth in the sight of mankind. And it leads astray the inhabitants of the earth, by reason of the signs which it was permitted to do in the sight of the beast, telling the inhabitants of the earth to make an image to the beast which has the wound of the sword, and yet lived. And it was permitted to give life to the image of the beast, that the image of the beast should both speak and cause that whoever would not worship the image of the beast should be killed. And it will cause all, the small and the great, and the rich and the poor, and the free and the bond, to have a mark on their right hand or on their foreheads, and it will bring it about that no one may be able to buy or sell, except him who has the mark, either the name of the beast or the number of its name.

"Here is wisdom. He who has understanding, let him calculate the number of the beast, for it is the number of a man; and its number is six hundred and sixty-six."[11] (13:1-18).

The Lamb and the Virgins; the Judgment (14:1-20)

John beholds the Lamb standing upon Mount Sion, and with Him 144,000 having His name and the name of His Father written on their foreheads; "These are they who were not defiled with women; for they are virgins. These follow the Lamb wherever He goes." (14:4).

Three angels appear in the heavens. The first proclaims that the hour of judgment has come. The second tells of the fall of Babylon (pagan Rome), while the third foretells the doom of all who worship the beast.

A voice from Heaven[12] is heard saying, "Write: Blessed are the dead who die in the Lord henceforth. Yes, says the Spirit, let them rest from their labors, for their works follow them." (14:13).

Upon a cloud is seen "one sitting like to a son of man, having upon his head a crown of gold and in his hand a sharp sickle." (14:14). He casts his sickle upon the earth and the earth is reaped.

An angel also appears with a sickle, and when he casts it to earth he gathers the vintage of the earth and casts it into the wine press of the wrath of God.

The Seven Bowls (15:1-8, 16:1-21)

Those who have overcome the beast stand upon a sea of glass mingled with fire, singing in triumph the song of Moses and the song of the Lamb.

Seven angels come forth from "the temple of the tabernacle of the testimony" which is opened in Heaven. They are given seven golden bowls "full of the wrath of God." A voice from the temple commands them: "Go and pour out the seven bowls of the wrath of God upon the earth." (16:1).

"And the first went and poured out his bowl upon the earth, and a sore and grievous wound was made upon the men who have the mark of the beast, and upon those who worshiped its image.

"And the second poured out his bowl upon the sea, and it became blood as of a dead man; and every live thing in the sea died.

"And the third poured out his bowl upon the rivers and fountains of waters, and they became blood . . .

"And the fourth poured out his bowl upon the sun, and he was allowed to scorch mankind with fire. And mankind was scorched with great heat, and they blasphemed the name of God who has authority over these plagues, and they did not repent and give Him glory.

"And the fifth poured out his bowl upon the throne of the beast; and its kingdom became dark, and they gnawed their tongues for pain. And they blasphemed the God of heaven because of their pains and wounds, and they did not repent of their works.

"And the sixth poured out his bowl upon the great river Euphrates, and dried up its waters, that a way might be made ready for the kings of the rising sun.

"And I saw issuing from the mouth of the dragon, and from the mouth of the beast, and from the mouth of the false prophet, three unclean spirits like frogs. For they are spirits of demons working signs, and they go forth unto the kings of the whole earth to gather them together for the battle on the great day of God almighty. 'Behold,[12] I come as a thief! Blessed is he who watches and keeps his garments, lest he walk naked and they see his shame.' And he gathered them together in a place that is called in Hebrew Armagedon.[13]

"And the seventh poured out his bowl upon the air, and there came forth a loud voice out of the temple from the throne, saying, 'It has come to pass!' And there were flashes of lightning, rumblings and peals of thunder, and there was a great earthquake such as never has been since men were first upon the earth, so great an earthquake was it. And the great city came into three parts; and the cities of the nations fell. And Babylon the great was remembered before God, to give her the cup of the wine of His fierce wrath. And every island fled away, and the mountains could not be found. And great hail, heavy as a talent, came down from heaven upon men; and men blasphemed God because of the plague of hail; for it was very great." (16:2-21).

The Woman on the Scarlet Beast (17:1-17)

"And there came one of the seven angels who had the seven bowls, and he spoke with me, saying 'Come, I will show thee the condemnation of the great harlot who sits upon many waters, with whom the kings of the earth have committed fornication, and the inhabitants of the earth were made drunk with the wine of her immorality.'

"And he took me away in spirit into a desert. And I saw a woman[14] sitting upon a scarlet-covered beast,[15] full of names of blasphemy, having seven heads and ten horns. And the woman was clothed in purple and scarlet, and covered with gold and precious stones and pearls, having in her hand a golden cup full of abominations and the uncleanness of her immorality. And upon her forehead a name written—a mystery—Babylon the great, the mother of the harlotries and of the abominations of the earth. And I saw the woman drunk with the blood of the saints and with the blood of the martyrs of Jesus. And when I saw her, I wondered with a great wonder.

"And the angel said to me, 'Wherefore dost thou wonder? I will tell thee the mystery of the woman, and of the beast that carries her which has the seven heads and the ten horns. The beast that thou sawest was, and is not, and is about to come up from the abyss, and will go to destruction.[16] And the inhabitants of the earth—whose names have not been written in the book of life from the foundation of the world—will wonder when they see the beast which was, and is not. And here is the meaning for him who has wisdom. The seven heads are seven mountains upon which the woman sits; and they are seven kings; five of them have fallen,[17] one is,[18] and the other has not yet come; and when he comes, he must remain a short time.[19] And the beast that was, and is not, is moreover himself eighth, and is of the seven, and is on his way to destruction.[20]

"'And the ten horns that thou sawest are ten kings[21] who have not received a kingdom as yet, but they will receive authority as kings for one hour, with the beast. These have one purpose and their power and authority they give to the beast. These will fight with the Lamb, and the Lamb will overcome them, for He is the Lord of lords, and the King of kings, and they who are with Him, called, and chosen, and faithful.'

"And he said to me, 'The waters that thou sawest where the harlot sits, are peoples and nations and tongues. And the ten horns that thou sawest, and the beast, these will hate the harlot, and will make her desolate and naked, and will eat her flesh, and will burn her up in fire. For God has put it into their hearts to carry out His purpose, to give their kingdom to the beast, until the words of God are accomplished. And the woman whom thou sawest is the great

city which has kingship over the kings of the earth.'"
(17:1-17).

The Fall of Babylon (18:1-24, 19:1-10)

An angel declares the fall of Babylon while a voice from
Heaven commands the faithful to leave the sinful city.

The kings of the earth, who committed fornication with
Babylon, lament her downfall. Dirges are also heard from
the merchants and mariners who have lost in her a rich
source of revenue.

An angel promises that Babylon will be overthrown with
the violence of a millstone cast into the sea. A triumphant
song, celebrating God's judgment on the harlot, is heard in
the heavens.

Defeat of the Beast and the False Prophet (19:11-21)

Christ appears, mounted on a white charger, followed by
the armies of Heaven. They give battle to the beast and the
kings of the earth with their armies. The latter are defeated.
The beast and the false prophet (the beast of the earth) are
seized and cast into the pool of fire and brimstone. Their
armies are killed by the sword of Him who sits upon the
horse.

Satan Chained (20:1-10)

"And I saw an angel coming down from heaven, having
the key of the abyss and a great chain in his hand. And he
laid hold on the dragon, the ancient serpent, who is the
devil and Satan, and bound him for a thousand years. And
he cast him into the abyss, and closed and sealed it over

him, that he should deceive the nations no more, until the thousand years should be finished. And after that he must be let loose for a little while.

"And I saw thrones, and men sat upon them and judgment was given to them. And I saw the souls of those who had been beheaded because of the witness to Jesus and because of the word of God, and who did not worship the beast or his image, and did not accept his mark upon their foreheads or upon their hands. And they came to life and reigned with Christ a thousand years. The rest of the dead did not come to life till the thousand years were finished. This is the first resurrection. Blessed and holy is he who has part in the first resurrection! Over these the second death has no power; but they will be priests of God and Christ, and will reign with Him a thousand years.[22]

"And when the thousand years are finished, Satan will be released from his prison, and will go forth and deceive the nations which are in the four corners of the earth, Gog and Magog,[23] and will gather them together for the battle; the number of whom is as the sand of the sea. And they went over the breadth of the earth and encompassed the camp of the saints, and the beloved city. And fire from God came down out of heaven and devoured them. And the devil who deceived them was cast into the pool of fire and brimstone, where are also the beast and the false prophet; and they will be tormented day and night forever and ever." (20:1-10).

Conclusion (20:11-15, 21:1-27, 22:1-21)

John witnesses the last judgment, then sees "a new heaven and a new earth." (These will be treated in the next chapter.)

The Apocalypse closes with the words of Christ: "Behold, I come quickly! And my reward is with Me, to render to each one according to his works. I am the Alpha and the Omega, the first and the last, the beginning and the end . . . I, Jesus, have sent My angel to testify to you these things concerning the churches . . . It is true, I come quickly!" (22:12-13, 16-20).

Saint John adds: "Amen! Come, Lord Jesus! The grace of Our Lord Jesus Christ be with all. Amen." (22:21).

NOTES

1. This is the Church of the Old and the New Covenants; it is probably only by accommodation that this text is applied to Our Blessed Lady.
2. In verse 9 the dragon is identified as Satan; some have seen here an indication that one third of the angels fell.
3. This is the third mention in the Apocalypse of three and one half years.
4. Here the vision takes us back to the beginning of time when Michael and the faithful angels drove Lucifer and the rebel angels from Heaven.
5. This is the fourth mention of three and one half years, this time using the exact terminology of the book of Daniel.
6. I.e., all faithful Christians.
7. This beast is thought to be (a) Imperial Rome; (b) the Antichrist.
8. This is the fifth mention of three and one half years.
9. Faith and patience are the weapons of the saints; they must be willing to accept suffering and death as Christ did.
10. This second beast may be (a) a false prophet; (b) the pagan priesthood that promulgated emperor-worship; (c) the political power that will support Antichrist.
11. For nearly nineteen hundred years men have been trying to solve the riddle in numerology posed here by St. John, though it must have been clearer to the early Christians than it is to us. Commentators are generally agreed that the number refers back to the beast of the sea, rather than to the beast of the earth, and the two most widely accepted interpretations are as follows: (a) to the Jews the number seven was the number of perfection (in the Apocalypse itself we find the Seven Spirits before the Throne, the Seven Letters to the Seven Churches, the Book with the Seven Seals, the Seven Angels with the Seven Trumpets, the Seven Bowls, etc.); consequently, the number six was considered imperfect since it fell just short of perfection. To write the

number six three times and then refer it to a man was to denote extreme imperfection in that man; (b) Hebrew letters also have a numerical value and the name Nero Caesar written in Hebrew adds up to 666. Nero was a type of the Antichrist, and when the latter appears, it is believed the number will have a mystic application to him also.

12. The voice of Christ.

13. The mountain of Megiddo, but more particularly the plain of Esdraelon which was the great battlefield of Palestine. Here the fortunes of kings were decided, so it has become a symbol of the place of supreme conflict between the forces of Good and Evil.

14. Pagan Rome, and perhaps the kingdom of Antichrist.

15. The beast is generally identified with the beast of the sea, ch. 13.

16. There was a widely held belief among early Christians that Nero was not dead, and that he would return to reign and persecute the Church again. This legend of "Nero redivivus" has already been hinted at in 13:3 in the first appearance of the beast of the sea: "And one of its heads was smitten, as it were, unto death; but its deadly wound was healed." St. John returns to that popular belief here and in the verses that follow.

17. I.e., Augustus, Tiberius, Caligula, Claudius and Nero.

18. Vespasian: some claim the Apocalypse was written in his reign; others hold that here St. John takes the prophecy backwards in time to his reign.

19. Titus.

20. Domitian: John makes use of the "Nero coming again" legend to point up the fact that Domitian comes in the spirit of Nero, and the Antichrist will come in the spirit of both.

21. Vassal rulers under the supremacy of Rome; also ten kings or rulers who will support Antichrist.

22. This is one of the most difficult passages in Scripture. Almost all commentators are now agreed that the thousand years is not to be taken literally, but simply to denote a long period of time. If the time sequence here is continuous and the beast (19:19) understood to be Antichrist, it would appear that after the latter's defeat the Church will enjoy a long era of peace and prosperity before the unchaining of Satan, another terrible assault from the powers of darkness, and finally the end of the world. Much more probable would seem the opinion that the beast here is understood to be the Roman empire. When it was conquered by the Church, the "millennium" began with the extension of Christ's kingdom through the world, aided by the prayers of the saints reigning in glory with Christ. It will end with the unchaining of Satan at the end of time and the giving of his full power

to the Antichrist.

The expression "first resurrection" then refers to the present state of the Church Triumphant in Heaven. The "second death" refers to eternal damnation.

23. Figurative names—found in rabbinical literature—used to designate the nations that will make the final onslaught against the Church.

Chapter 13

THE LAST JUDGMENT

Suddenness of Christ's Coming

"For as the lightning comes forth from the east and shines even to the west, so also will the coming of the Son of Man be." (*Matt.* 24:27; also *Luke* 17:24).

". . . the day of the Lord is to come as a thief in the night. For when they shall say 'Peace and security,' even then sudden destruction will come upon them, as birth pangs upon her who is with child, and they will not escape." (1 *Thess.* 5:2-3).

Resurrection of the Dead

"For I know that my Redeemer liveth, and in the last day I shall rise out of the earth. And I shall be clothed again with my skin, and in my flesh I shall see my God . . ." (*Job* 19:25-26).

"And many of those that sleep in the dust of the earth, shall awake; some unto life everlasting, and others unto reproach, to see it always." (*Daniel* 12:2).

"Amen, amen, I say to you, the hour is coming, and now is here, when the dead shall hear the voice of the Son of God, and those who hear shall live." (*John* 5:25).

113

". . . the hour is coming in which all who are in the tombs shall hear the voice of the Son of God. And they who have done good shall come forth unto resurrection of life; but they who have done evil unto resurrection of judgment." (*John* 5:28-29).

"Behold, I tell you a mystery: we shall indeed rise, but we shall not all be changed[1]—in a moment, in the twinkling of an eye, at the last trumpet. For the trumpet shall sound, and the dead shall rise incorruptible and we shall be changed. For this corruptible body must put on incorruption, and this mortal body must put on immortality. But when this mortal body puts on immortality, then shall come to pass the word that is written, 'Death is swallowed up in victory! O death, where is thy victory? O death, where is thy sting?'" (1 *Corinth.* 15:51-55).

". . . we who live, who survive until the coming of the Lord, shall not precede those who have fallen asleep. For the Lord Himself with cry of command, with voice of archangel, and with trumpet of God will descend from heaven; and the dead in Christ will rise up first. Then we who live, who survive, shall be caught up together with them in clouds to meet the Lord in the air, and so we shall ever be with the Lord." (1 *Thess.* 4:15-17).

Place of Judgment

"I will gather together all nations, and will bring them down into the valley of Josaphat . . ." (*Joel* 3:2).

". . . let the nations come up into the valley of Josaphat, for there I will sit to judge all nations round about." (*Joel* 3:12).

Role of the Angels

". . . the harvest is the end of the world and the reapers are the angels . . . The Son of Man will send forth His angels, and they will gather out of His kingdom all scandals, and those who work iniquity, and cast them into the furnace of fire, where there will be weeping, and the gnashing of teeth." (*Matt.* 13:39, 41-42).

"So will it be at the end of the world. The angels will go out and separate the wicked from among the just, and will cast them into the furnace of fire . . ." (*Matt.* 13:49-50).

". . . they will see the Son of Man coming upon the clouds of heaven with great power and majesty. And He will send forth His angels with a trumpet and a great sound, and they will gather His elect from the four winds, from one end of the heavens to the other." (*Matt.* 24:30-31; also *Mark* 13:26-27).

Role of the Apostles

"Amen I say to you that you who have followed me, in the regeneration when the Son of Man shall sit on the throne of His glory, shall also sit on twelve thrones, judging the twelve tribes of Israel." (*Matt.* 19:28).

The Last Judgment

". . . we shall all stand at the judgment-seat of God." (*Romans* 14:10).

"Nevertheless, I say to you, hereafter you shall see the Son of Man sitting at the right hand of the Power and coming upon the clouds of heaven." (*Matt.* 26:64; also *Mark* 14:62).

"For the Son of Man is to come with His angels in the glory of His Father, and then He will render to everyone according to his conduct." (*Matt.* 16:27).

"And I say to you, everyone who acknowledges Me before men, him will the Son of Man also acknowledge before the angels of God. But whoever disowns Me before men will be disowned before the angels of God." (*Luke* 12:8-9).

"For whoever is ashamed of Me and My words, of him will the Son of Man be ashamed when He comes in His glory and that of the Father and of the holy angels." (*Luke* 9:26; also *Mark* 8:38).

"But when the Son of Man shall come in His majesty, and all the angels with Him, then He will sit on the throne of His glory; and before Him will be gathered all the nations, and He will separate them one from another, as the shepherd separates the sheep from the goats; and He will set the sheep on His right hand, but the goats on the left.

"Then the King will say to those on His right hand, 'Come, blessed of My Father, take possession of the kingdom prepared for you from the foundation of the world; for I was hungry and you gave Me to eat; I was thirsty and you gave Me to drink; I was a stranger and you took Me in; naked and you covered Me; sick and you visited Me; I was in prison and you came to Me.' Then the just will answer Him, saying, 'Lord, when did we see Thee hungry, and feed Thee; or thirsty, and give Thee drink? And when did we see Thee a stranger, and take Thee in; or naked, and clothe Thee? Or when did we see Thee sick, or in prison, and come to Thee?' And answering the King will say to them, 'Amen I say to you, as long as you did it for one of these, the least of My brethren, you did it for Me.'

"Then He will say to those on His left hand, 'Depart from Me, accursed ones, into the everlasting fire which was prepared for the devil and his angels. For I was hungry, and you did not give Me to eat; I was thirsty and you gave Me no drink; I was a stranger and you did not take Me in; naked, and you did not clothe Me; sick, and in prison, and you did not visit Me.' Then they will also answer and say, 'Lord, when did we see Thee hungry, or thirsty, or a stranger, or naked, or sick, or in prison, and did not minister to Thee?' Then He will answer them, saying, 'Amen I say to you, as long as you did not do it for one of these least ones, you did not do it for Me.' And these will go into everlasting punishment, but the just into everlasting life." (*Matt.* 25:31-46).

"And I saw a great white throne and the one who sat upon it; from His face the earth and heaven fled away, and there was found no place for them. And I saw the dead, the great and the small, standing before the throne, and scrolls were opened. And another scroll was opened, which is the book of life; and the dead were judged out of those things that were written in the scrolls, according to their works. And the sea gave up the dead that were in it, and death and hell gave up the dead that were in them; and they were judged each one, according to their works.

"And hell and death were cast into the pool of fire. This is the second death, the pool of fire. And if anyone was not found written in the book of life, he was cast into the pool of fire." (*Apoc.* 20:11-15).

Final Condemnation of the Fallen Angels

"For God did not spare the angels when they sinned, but

dragged them down by infernal ropes to Tartarus, and delivered them to be tortured and kept in custody for judgment." (2 *Peter* 2:4).

"And the angels also who did not preserve their original state, but forsook their abode, He has kept in everlasting chains under darkness for the judgment of the great day." (*Jude* 6).

"Do you not know that the saints will judge the world?[2] . . . Do you not know that we shall judge angels?" (1 *Corinth.* 6:2-3).

Eternal State of the Just

"But they that are learned[3] shall shine as the brightness of the firmament, and they that instruct many to justice, as stars for all eternity." (*Dan.* 12:3).

". . . the just shall shine forth like the sun in the kingdom of their Father." (*Matt.* 13:43).

"There is one glory of the sun, and another glory of the moon, and another of the stars; for star differs from star in glory. So also with the resurrection of the dead. What is sown in corruption rises in incorruption; what is sown in dishonor rises in glory; what is sown in weakness rises in power; what is sown a natural body rises a spiritual body." (1 *Corinth.* 15:41-44).

"For at the resurrection they will neither marry nor be given in marriage, but will be as angels of God in heaven." (*Matt.* 22:30; also *Mark* 12:25).

"But those who shall be accounted worthy of that world[4]

and of the resurrection from the dead, neither marry nor take wives. For neither shall they be able to die any more, for they are equal to the angels, and are sons of God, being sons of the resurrection." (*Luke* 20:35-36).

New Heaven and New Earth

"For behold I create new heavens, and a new earth; and the former things shall not be in remembrance, and they shall not come upon the heart." (*Isaias* 65:17).

"But we look for new heavens and a new earth, according to His promises, wherein dwells justice." (2 *Peter* 3:13).

"And I saw a new heaven and a new earth. For the first heaven and the first earth had passed away, and the sea is no more. And I saw the holy city, New Jerusalem, coming down out of heaven from God, made ready as a bride adorned for her husband. And I heard a loud voice from the throne saying, 'Behold the dwelling of God with men, and He will dwell with them. And they will be His people, and God Himself will be with them as their God. And God will wipe away every tear from their eyes. And death shall be no more; neither shall there be mourning, nor crying, nor pain any more, for the former things have passed away.'

"And He who was sitting on the throne said, 'Behold, I make all things new!' And He said, 'Write, for these words are trustworthy and true.' And He said to me, 'It is done! I am the Alpha and the Omega, the beginning and the end. To him who thirsts I will give of the fountain of the water of life freely. He who overcomes shall possess these things, and I will be his God, and he shall be My son. But as for the cowardly and unbelieving, and abominable and murderers, and fornicators and sorcerers, and idolaters and all liars, their portion shall be in the pool that burns with fire and brimstone, which is the second death.'" (*Apoc.* 21:1-8).

The Heavenly Jerusalem

"And there came one of the seven angels who had the bowls full of the seven last plagues; and he spoke with me, saying, 'Come, I will show thee the bride, the spouse of the Lamb.' And he took me up in spirit to a mountain, great and high, and showed me the holy city Jerusalem coming down out of heaven from God, having the glory of God. Its light was like to a precious stone, as it were a jasper-stone, clear as crystal. And it had a wall great and high with twelve gates, and at the gates twelve angels, and names written on them, which are the names of the twelve tribes of the children of Israel. On the east are three gates, and on the north three gates, and on the south three gates, and on the west three gates. And the wall of the city has twelve foundation stones, and on them twelve names of the apostles of the Lamb.

"And he who spoke with me had a measure, a golden reed, to measure the city and the gates thereof and the wall. And the city stands four-square, and its length is as great as its breadth; and he measured the city with the reed, to twelve thousand stadia: the length and the breadth and the height of it are equal. And he measured its wall, of a hundred and forty-four cubits, man's measure, that is, angel's measure.[5] And the material of its wall was jasper; but the city itself was pure gold, like pure glass. And the foundations of the wall of the city were adorned with every precious stone. The first foundation, jasper; the second, sapphire; the third, agate; the fourth, emerald; the fifth, sardonyx; the sixth, sardius; the seventh, chrysolite; the eighth, beryl; the ninth, topaz; the tenth, chrysoprase; the eleventh, jacinth; the twelfth, amethyst. And the twelve gates were twelve pearls; that is, each gate was of a single pearl. And the street of the city was pure gold, as it were transparent glass.

"And I saw no temple therein. For the Lord God almighty and the Lamb are the temple thereof. And the city has no need of the sun or the moon to shine upon it. For the glory of God lights it up, and the Lamb is the lamp thereof. And the nations shall walk by the light thereof; and the kings of the earth shall bring their glory and honor into it. And its gates shall not be shut by day; for there shall be no night there. And they shall bring the glory and the honor of nations into it. And there shall not enter anything defiled, nor he who practices abomination and falsehood, but those only who are written in the book of life of the Lamb.

"And he showed me a river of the water of life, clear as crystal coming forth from the throne of God and of the Lamb. In the midst of the city street, on both sides of the river, was the tree of life, bearing twelve fruits, yielding its fruit according to each month, and the leaves for the healing of the nations.

"And there shall be no more any accursed thing; but the throne of God and of the Lamb shall be in it, and His servants shall serve Him. And they shall see His face and His name shall be on their foreheads. And night shall be no more, and they shall have no need of light of lamp, or light of sun, for the Lord God will shed light upon them; and they shall reign forever and ever." (*Apoc.* 21:9-27; 22:1-5).

NOTES

1. This implies that those living on the last day shall not die.
2. The elect will concur in the sentence pronounced by Christ.
3. I.e., learned in the knowing and keeping of God's law.
4. Heaven.
5. The measure of a man, but the reed is handled by an angel.

APPENDIX A

The Complete Prophecy of Saint Malachy

(Asterisks denote anti-popes.)

1. "From a Castle on the Tiber"... Celestine II (1143-1144)
2. "The Enemy Routed"............ Lucius II (1144-1145)
3. "Of the Highest Mountain" .. Bl. Eugene III (1145-1153)
4. "The Suburran Abbot"....... Anastasius IV (1153-1154)
5. "From the White Country" ...... Adrian IV (1154-1159)
6. "Out of the Loathsome Prison".. *Victor IV (1159-1164)
7. "Road on the Further Side
     of the Tiber".............. *Paschal III (1164-1168)
8. "From the Hungary
     of Tusculum" .... *Callistus III (1168-1178)
9. "From the Watchful Goose" .. Alexander III (1159-1181)
10. "Light in the Gate"............. Lucius III (1181-1185)
11. "The Sow in the Sieve".......... Urban III (1185-1187)
12. "Sword of Lawrence" .... Gregory VIII (1187-1187)
13. "He Will Come Out of
     the School"................. Clement III (1187-1191)
14. "From the Animal Country"... Celestine III (1191-1198)
15. "A Signed Count" .... Innocent III (1198-1216)
16. "A Canon from the Side" .... Honorious III (1216-1227)
17. "The Bird of Ostia" .... Gregory IX (1227-1241)
18. "The Sabine Lion" .... Celestine IV (1241-1241)
19. "Count Lawrence"............. Innocent IV (1243-1254)
20. "Sign of Ostia".............. Alexander IV (1254-1261)
21. "Jerusalem of Champagne"....... Urban IV (1261-1264)
22. "The Crushed Dragon" .... Clement IV (1265-1268)
23. "The Snake-man"........... Bl. Gregory X (1271-1276)
24. "The French Preacher" ..... Bl. Innocent V (1276-1276)
25. "The Good Count".............. Adrian V (1276-1276)
26. "The Tusculan Fisherman" ...... John XXI (1276-1277)
27. "A Well-formed Rose" .... Nicholas III (1277-1280)

65. "The Flower of the Pill
      for the Sick".............Clement VII (1523-1534)
66. "The Hyacinth of the Physician" ... Paul III (1534-1549)
67. "Of the Mountain Crown"........Julius III (1550-1555)
68. "The Weak Grain" ....Marcellus II (1555-1555)
69. "Of the Faith of Peter"............Paul IV (1555-1559)
70. "The Medicine of Aesculapius" ....Pius IV (1559-1565)
71. "The Angel of the Wood" ....St. Pius V (1566-1572)
72. "A Half-body of the Balls" ...Gregory XIII (1572-1585)
73. "The Axis in the
      Midst of the Sign" ....Sixtus V (1585-1590)
74. "Of the Heavenly Dew"........Urban VII (1590-1590)
75. "From the Old City" ....Gregory XIV (1590-1591)
76. "A Pious City in War" ....Innocent IX (1591-1591)
77. "Cross of Romulus".........Clement VIII (1592-1605)
78. "Man of the Waves"...............Leo XI (1605-1605)
79. "A Perverse Race" ....Paul V (1605-1621)
80. "In the Tribulation of Peace" ..Gregory XV (1621-1623)
81. "The Lily and the Rose".......Urban VIII (1623-1644)
82. "The Joy of the Cross"........Innocent X (1644-1655)
83. "The Guardian of
      the Mountains".........Alexander VII (1655-1667)
84. "The Star of the Swans" ....Clement IX (1667-1669)
85. "Of the Great River"...........Clement X (1670-1676)
86. "The Insatiable Beast" ....Innocent XI (1676-1689)
87. "Glorious Penance"........Alexander VIII (1689-1691)
88. "Portcullis in the Gate".......Innocent XII (1691-1700)
89. "The Encircling Flowers"......Clement XI (1700-1721)
90. "Of the Good
      Religious Order"........Innocent XIII (1721-1724)
91. "A Soldier at War"..........Benedict XIII (1724-1730)
92. "The Lofty Column...........Clement XII (1730-1740)
93. "A Rural Animal"...........Benedict XIV (1740-1758)
94. "The Rose of Umbria".......Clement XIII (1758-1769)
95. "The Nimble Bear"..........Clement XIV (1769-1774)
96. "The Apostolic Wanderer".........Pius VI (1775-1799)
97. "The Rapacious Eagle"...........Pius VII (1800-1823)
98. "The Dog and the Serpent".......Leo XII (1823-1829)
99. "A Religious Man"..............Pius VIII (1829-1830)
100. "From Balnea in Etruria".....Gregory XVI (1831-1846)
101. "Cross from a Cross"..............Pius IX (1846-1878)
102. "Light in the Heavens" ....Leo XIII (1878-1903)
103. "Burning Fire".................St. Pius X (1903-1914)

104. "Religion Devastated" .... Benedict XV (1914-1922)
105. "Intrepid Faith" .... Pius XI (1922-1939)
106. "The Angelic Shepherd" .... Pius XII (1939-1958)
107. "The Shepherd
         and the Sailor" .... John XXIII (1958-1963)
108. "Flower of Flowers" .... Paul VI (1963-1978)
109. "From the Half of the Moon" ... John Paul I (1978-1978)
110. "From the Labor of the Sun" .. John Paul II (1978-   )
111. "From the Glory of the Olive"

In the final persecution of the Holy Roman Church there
shall reign Peter the Roman who will feed his flock amid
many tribulations, after which the seven-hilled city will be
destroyed and the terrible judge will judge the people.

APPENDIX B

Apparitions Since Fatima

Because of the extraordinary prophecies given at Fatima, the faithful have manifested great interest in apparitions reported since 1917 to see if Our Lady has amended or added to the Fatima predictions in any way. There have been reports of 30 to 50 such apparitions all over the world in recent years—and specifically from 1931. Of these, the Church has approved only those of Beauraing (1932-1933) and Banneux (1933). The short messages given in these apparitions have already been given in chapter six of this book. As far as we know, no prophecies were made. It is true that several of the children were given secrets, but it would appear that they were of a personal nature, similar to those given to Saint Bernadette at Lourdes.

In all other apparitions reported since 1931, the Church has given a negative decision or no decision at all, so the public should be wary in all reading on such. The Holy Office in Rome has warned the faithful against a too ready acceptance of reports of supernatural phenomena, and the replacing of true devotion with a love of the sensational.

APPENDIX C

Can the Devil Raise the Dead?

Mr. Frederick Kaigh in *Witchcraft and Magic of Africa* describes his personal observations in South Africa and Rhodesia in the 1930s. There is no reason to doubt any of his statements of fact. We reproduce here his account of the restoration of life to the corpse of a murdered native chief. Despite the impressiveness of the occurrence, it will be apparent that the chief was not returned to life in the sense that Christ gave life back to Lazarus or the widow's son. In true restorations, the person raised from the dead continues a normal life among men. In false restorations, there is no evidence that the soul has been restored to the corpse in anything like its true natural relationship, nor even any evidence that the spirit using the corpse is the soul which originally animated it.

Mr. Kaigh, who was the government physician at the time, was sent to investigate the cause and circumstances of the death of Chief Nkatosi. The headmen at the chief's kraal informed him the chief was already buried, and sought to thus terminate the matter. Using his governmental authority, he insisted on opening the grave, and did so. He found that the body was, indeed, in a grave that appeared filled in, but in fact, was merely camouflaged to appear so. While he had the body brought to the surface despite the protests of the natives, Lokanzi, the nyanga (witch doctor), squatted at the graveside in a trance.

The body had been laid on one blanket and covered with another. The English doctor could see it clearly outlined under the blanket and had felt it through the blanket as he was helping get it out of the grave. Moreover, the stench was awful. He set out his instruments for an autopsy, reached over and pulled the top blanket back. There was no body there, just a spot of dried blood and brains where the head had rested.

The physician then by shouts and threats brought the nyanga out of his trance, and after some argument, received this message from Lokanzi, standing as in a trance: "Nkatosi's spirit tells me that mortal hands shall not touch his body until he shall be finished with it tonight." The physician agreed not to touch the body, but demanded to see it. Lokanzi, again in a trance, replied, "The spirit of Nkatosi sees your heart. It is good. You can see my body, but I must take it away if it be touched."

This time the physician insisted that Lokanzi pull back the blanket. The nyanga leaned over the blankets and spoke as if to the dead man but in the secret tongue of the witch doctors. He did not touch the blanket at any time. After his words over the blanket, he straightened up. The top blanket was pulled back in a manner that could not be explained and under it was Nkatosi's corpse.

The physician noted a horrible hole in the skull, and beneath the hole, the dried blood and brains. He did not touch the body, but he announced that he would attend the ceremony that evening in which Nkatosi was said to need his body. All three were there: physician, nyanga and the corpse. It was called a propitiation ceremony.

The kraal was first given an actual and a ceremonial cleaning, and on each house, witch-doctor medicine was hung. All trace of ash or burnt wood was carefully removed.

The chief's throne was placed on skins in the open with its back to where the moon would be. The personal belongings of the dead man were around the throne. Great quantities of food and beer were gathered so that all could feast.

Food especially liked by the chief was set near the throne.

Darkness came, and the moon moved into position. All the men of the tribe, but no women, were present. Drums began to beat, but it was not possible to locate them from the sound.

Lokanzi, the witch doctor, was sitting before the throne drinking some of his own medicine. He appeared to be in a trance. Then, rising, he began to speak in the secret language of his calling. The physician was given to understand that he was praising the dead chief to please the spirit so it would surely return.

A little fire had been made of specially cut wood and was burning brightly as the witch doctor spoke. He then threw something into the flames, which burned with various colors and gave off a pungent scent and a heavy cloud of smoke, which circulated in its own way without regard to the wind. Even at a distance, it gave one the feeling of being a little drunk.

The nyanga was not very clearly visible in the smoke, but one thing he was clearly seen to do. He stuck a curious stick in the ground. At the top was a fair figure of a human head made of skin that looked human, and there was a tuft of human hair sewed on top.

Lokanzi suddenly let out an unearthly howl, the drums began softly and the nyanga went into a dance. The drums became louder and louder, and then went into a fierce rhythm as the dance became wilder and wilder. Froth, blood and sweat poured from the dancer's body. At the height of this mad dance, Lokanzi fell, as if dead, in a trance and all was silence. In a few seconds, there was a great shout from the crowd, and all were sitting and clapping, the royal salute. And Chief Nkatosi was sitting on his throne.

He spoke: "I see you, people." It was his natural voice. They answered, "Chief, we see you."

Then three times, the chief addressed Lokanzi, but the

witch doctor did not answer or move. Then in the sight of all, the stick with the human-like head moved across in front of the throne and disappeared into the witch doctor's body. He sat up wearily, and the chief addressed him a fourth time. He acknowledged the greeting and invited the chief to eat and drink. The dead man took the dipper and drank. Then with his fingers, he began to eat from the bowl. Everyone else also began to eat—even the English physician who was unable not to do so and who later could not recall the taste of the food.

While eating and drinking, the dead chief and his witch doctor carried on a normal conversation. Afterward, the chief spoke to all the people clearly and intelligently. He designated his rightful successor, named his murderer and described the way in which he would now leave them. When he finished his speech, he took one last dipper of beer. He then raised up from his throne and stepped off the skins onto the ground. He turned away from the people to face the moon, and as he did so, the gash in his head could be seen. He walked slowly and regally down a lane in the moonlight and was seen no more.

The physician, who acted also as a police officer, dispatched his lieutenant to find the man named as the murderer. He was found by morning, quite dead, and neither the government physician nor others called in could discover any cause of death. (Condensed from pages 50 to 64 of the book referred to above and published in 1947 by Richard Leslie and Co., London.)

BIBLIOGRAPHY

The Holy Bible: Old Testament, Douay Version; New Testament, Confraternity Version

The New Testament—Knox

The New Testament—Spencer

A Catholic Commentary on Holy Scripture (Nelson)

Commentary on the New Testament (Catholic Biblical Association)

The Apostolic Fathers (Cima)

Catholic Encyclopedia: articles on Antichrist, Apocalypse, Eschatology, La Salette, Prophecy

Biver: *Pere Lamy* (TAN Books and Publishers)

Culleton: *Prophets and Our Times; Reign of Antichrist* (TAN Books and Publishers)

de Marchi: *Crusade of Fatima*

Emmerich: *Life of Christ* (TAN Books and Publishers)

Forman: *Story of Prophecy*

Gillett: *Shrines of Our Lady*

Kondor: *Fatima in Lucia's Own Words*

Martindale: *Antichrist; Meaning of Fatima*

McGlynn: *Vision of Fatima*

Oca: *More about Fatima*

Pelletier: *The Sun Danced at Fatima*

Pohle-Preuss: *Eschatology*

Saint Thomas Aquinas: *Summa Theologica; In Ommes S. Pauli Ap. Epistolae Commentaria*

Ullathorne: *Holy Mountain of La Salette*

Many articles on Eschatology, Prophecy, St. Malachy, Blessed Anna Maria Taigi, and Apparitions of Our Lady, in the following Catholic periodicals:

> *American Ecclesiastical Review*
> *Catholic Biblical Quarterly*
> *Catholic Digest*
> *Christian Family*
> *Denver Register*
> *Our Lady of the Cape*
> *Scapular*

If you have enjoyed this book, consider making your next selection from among the following . . .